mini AMIGURUMI made EASY

Mini Amigurumi Made Easy
25 Quick & Easy Animal Crochet Patterns
Mariska Vos-Bolman (DIY Fluffies)

Have you made characters with patterns from this book?
Share your creations on *www.amigurumi.com/5400*
or on Instagram with *#amigurumimadeeasy*

First published July 2025
by Meteoor BV, Antwerp, Belgium
www.meteoorbooks.com
hello@meteoorbooks.com

Text and step-by-step images: Mariska Vos-Bolman
Photography: Meteoor BV
Printed and bound by Grafistar

Yarn sponsor:

ISBN 978-949164-356-9
D/2025/13.531/2

A catalogue record for this book is available from the Royal Library of Belgium.

MARISKA VOS-BOLMAN
DIY FLUFFIES

25 quick and easy animal crochet patterns

METEOOR BOOKS

Hi! I'm Mariska! I am the designer and creator behind DIY Fluffies. I started designing toys in 2008, when I bought my first sewing machine and used it to make my first soft toy. About a year later, I taught myself how to crochet. My son received a cute rattle toy as a gift and it inspired me to try my hand at amigurumi crochet. **I started making a cute little cat ... and then promptly put it away somewhere in a box and left it unfinished for 6 years.** At that point in my life, the care for my young children and the work for my sewing business were taking up all of my time, and I simply didn't have any time to spare for other crafts, however much I wanted to try them. That little amigurumi cat stayed tucked away until I felt I had a little more time on my hands. **And when I finally took it out of the box to complete, it immediately sparked my desire to delve deep into the world of amigurumi toymaking.** I first practiced my skills by making other designers' patterns, and eventually gained the experience and confidence to start making my own designs as well.

I'd already made several pattern contributions to the popular *"Zoomigurumi"* crochet book series when Meteoor Books asked me to write my very own book. ***"Amigurumi Made Easy"* was published in 2023 and to my utmost joy, it reached lots of crocheters and became quite a bestseller.** *"Amigurumi Made Easy"* is a collection of cute and cuddly toys, written for beginners who want to start making fun amigurumi. In *"Mini Amigurumi Made Easy"*, I've adopted the same approach to my designs, using simple shapes and clear instructions to help crocheters make small amigurumi with ease. **These mini amigurumi are quick and easy to make and most can be worked up in just a few hours.** You can make all of them in a heavier yarn weight as well, such as worsted weight or bulky weight yarn, so you'll have a cuddly plushie in no time at all.

It brings me so much joy to see people bringing my patterns to life by making their own toys, or to hear from crocheters who began their creative journey with one of my designs. It was my childhood dream to have a career filled with creativity and joy, and through designing amigurumi, I feel like that dream has come true. I hope you'll enjoy making these mini animals just as much as I loved creating them!

Mariska

WHAT IS AMIGURUMI?

These toys are crocheted in the amigurumi style. The style originated in Japan and its meaning translates into English as a crocheted or knitted stuffed doll (in Japanese, *ami* means "crocheted" or "knitted" and *nuigurumi* means "stuffed doll"). Amigurumi are created by crocheting in a spiral, without joining in the round and without turning the crochetwork. This results in three-dimensional forms that can be sewn together to create a toy.

EVERYTHING YOU NEED

Yarn

For every pattern in this book, I've listed the yarn used to create the design. The yarn I work with is *Yarn and Colors Must-Have*, a 100% mercerized cotton, sport weight yarn. Cotton is one of the most used threads for crochet. This thread has practically no elasticity, which is favorable when making toys, so the final result keeps its shape. In addition to being a hypoallergenic, washable material, cotton is extremely durable, very soft, and available in lots of colors! For fun, I've also made some of the mini amigurumi in this book in chenille super bulky weight yarn. With this yarn weight, the toys turn out much bigger (and just as cute and cuddly).

> ***Tip:*** *If you're having a hard time working in sport weight yarn, don't hesitate to switch to a thicker yarn weight (and bigger crochet hook accordingly). The designs work up equally well in light worsted or worsted weight yarn and working with a thicker yarn weight can be a great way to boost your skills and confidence and help you work with sport weight yarn later. Just choose the yarn weight that feels good for you.*

Don't feel tied to my yarn choices though: any weight of cotton, acrylic or wool can be used as a substitute. If you change the yarn weight (thickness), you'll want to match the right crochet hook accordingly. Check the chart on page 9 for a quick comparison of yarn weights and corresponding recommended hook sizes.

> ***Note:*** *When crocheting amigurumi, use a slightly smaller hook than what's recommended on the yarn label. This way, your stitches will be tighter and the stuffing will not show through.*

The patterns state the yarn quantity. The amounts are rather small and will vary according to how loosely or tightly you crochet. You could use the remnants of other projects or start with a new ball of yarn. When more than one ball is needed, I mention this in the materials list.

Crochet hook

Hooks as well come in different sorts and sizes. Bigger hooks make bigger stitches than smaller ones. It's important to match the right hook size with the right yarn weight.
For amigurumi, you generally want to use a hook two or three sizes smaller than what is recommended on your yarn label. The crochet fabric should be quite tight, without any gaps through which the stuffing can escape. Using a smaller hook makes it easier to achieve this. Hooks are usually made from aluminum or steel. Metal hooks tend to slip between the stitches more easily. Preferably choose a crochet hook with a rubber ergonomic handle.

Stitch marker

A stitch marker is a small metal or plastic clip. It's a simple tool to mark your starting point and give you the assurance that you've made the right number of stitches in each round. Mark the last stitch of the round with your stitch marker. You move your stitch marker up one round at the end of each round.
When you reach your stitch marker after crocheting

a new round, you take it out, crochet in this stitch, then put it in the last stitch you crocheted.

> ***Note:*** *You could also use a leftover piece of yarn in a contrasting color as a stitch marker. If you're using a yarn tail as a stitch marker, remember to remove it when the toy is finished.*

Stuffing

For the filling, polyester fiberfill is advised. It's washable and non-allergenic.
The individual parts of a toy are stuffed while the piece is being crocheted. The stuffing of wider pieces such as the head or body begins when they are roughly half finished. For stuffing very thin pieces in which you cannot fit a finger, the back of a crochet hook or a chopstick can be used.
Generally, when stuffing a toy, it's important to use more stuffing than you might initially think. If the toy is not stuffed tightly, it will lose its shape over time. On the other hand, if it's over-stuffed, the stuffing may cause the fabric to stretch and become visible. You'll need to find the right balance.

my favorite

NUMBER (SYMBOL)	1	2	3	4	5	6
CATEGORY NAME	super fine	fine	light	medium	heavy	very heavy
UK YARN TYPE	3 ply	4 ply	double knitting (DK)	aran	chunky	super chunky
US YARN TYPE	Fingering	Sport	Light Worsted	Worsted	Bulky	Extra Bulky
THE HOOK I RECOMMEND IN US SIZE	8 steel to B-1	B-1	B-1 to E-4	E-4 to 7	7 to I-9	I-9 to K-10 1/2
THE HOOK I RECOMMEND IN METRIC SIZE	1.5 to 2.5mm	2 to 2.5mm	2.5 to 3.5mm	3.5 to 4.5mm	4.5 to 5.5mm	5.5 to 6.5mm

Safety eyes

For some of these designs, safety eyes are used. Safety eyes come in two different parts – the front (the bead that will show on the outside, on a ribbed stem) and the back (the washer). The washer keeps the eye in place. Be careful when you apply safety eyes: once you put the washer on, you won't be able to pull it off again, so make sure that the post is where you want it to be before attaching the washer.
If you're crocheting these toys for children under the age of three, it's advised to embroider the facial features for safety.

***Note**: Some of the patterns have embroidered eyes instead of safety eyes. You can embroider the eyes any way you like, I made them by taking a strand of black yarn on my tapestry needle and sewing a few times over 1-2 stitches for each eye.*

Tapestry needle

For embroidery, a tapestry needle with a rounded tip is used. This rounded tip makes it easier to insert your needle in a specific space without splitting your yarn.

Sewing pins

It can be handy to have some sewing pins lying around, to help position body parts before sewing them on permanently.

Keychain

If you want to turn your mini amigurumi into a cute keychain, you can insert the ring of the keychain into a top stitch of the amigurumi and close it with pliers.

PATTERN STRUCTURE

These patterns are worked in **continuous spirals**. Crocheting in spirals can be confusing since there's no clear indication of where a new round begins and the previous one ends. To keep track of the rounds, you can mark the end of a round with a stitch marker. After crocheting the next round, you should end up right above your stitch marker. Move your stitch marker at the end of each round to keep track of where you are.

At the beginning of each line you will find 'Rnd + a number' to indicate which round you are in. If a round is repeated, you'll read 'Rnd 9 – 12', for example. You then repeat this round four times, crocheting the stitches in round 9, 10, 11 and 12.

Although we usually crochet in rounds, occasionally it happens that we switch to **rows**, going back and forth instead of working in continuous spirals. When we switch to rows, it will be indicated with 'Row + a number'. You end the row with a ch 1 and turn your crochetwork to start the next. Don't count this turning chain as a stitch and skip it when working the next row (unless otherwise mentioned).

At the end of each line, you'll find the total number of stitches you should have in square brackets, for example [9]. When in doubt, take a moment to check your stitch count.

When parts of the instructions repeat throughout the round, we place them between rounded brackets, followed by the number of times this part should be worked. We do this to shorten the pattern and make it less cluttered.

COUNTING STITCHES

Counting stitches will help you ensure that you are following the pattern correctly. When counting stitches, you do not count the slip knot or the loop on the hook (this is the working loop). The easiest way to count stitches is to look at the plaited tops (V's at the top of your crochetwork).
If you discover you missed one stitch or made one too many, you can always try to correct it by making an (extra) increase or decrease in the following round.

ABBREVIATIONS

If this is your first time crocheting from a pattern, the abbreviations might feel like a foreign language. However, once you get used to decoding them, they actually make it easier to quickly decipher a pattern. This book is written using US crochet terms.

Rnd	round	slst	slip stitch
st	stitch	inc	increase
ch	chain	dec	decrease
sc	single crochet	BLO	back loops only
hdc	half double crochet	FLO	front loops only
dc	double crochet		

AMIGURUMI GALLERY

With each pattern, we have included a URL and QR code that will take you to that character's dedicated online gallery. Share your finished amigurumi, find inspiration in the color and yarn choices of your fellow crocheters and enjoy the fun of crocheting. Simply follow the link or scan the QR code with your mobile phone. Phones with iOS will scan the QR code automatically in camera mode. For phones with Android you may need to activate QR code scanning or install a separate QR Reader app.

PATTERN VIDEOS

I have created full video tutorials of a few of the mini amigurumi included in this book. You can find these, as well as other crochet resources, on *www.youtube.com/@DIYFluffies.*

STITCHES

If this is your first time making amigurumi, you might find it useful to have a tutorial at hand. With the stitches explained on the following pages, you can make all of the amigurumi in this book. I suggest you practice the basic stitches before you start making one of the designs. This will help you to read the patterns and abbreviations more comfortably, without having to browse back to these pages.
This book is written in US crochet terms.

STITCH TUTORIAL VIDEOS

With each stitch explanation I have included a URL and QR code that will take you to an online stitch tutorial video, showing the technique step by step to help you master it even more quickly. Simply follow the link or scan the QR code with your smartphone. Phones with iOS will scan the QR code automatically in camera mode. For phones with Android you may need to install a QR Reader app first.

HOLD THE HOOK AND YARN (HAND POSITION)

Usually, we handle the hook with the same hand we use to write, but it's not a rule. If you take it with your right hand, you will crochet from right to left. If you take it with your left hand, you will crochet from left to right.
There are different ways of holding a crochet hook. You will need to experiment and find the way that feels the most comfortable for you.

Pencil grip

Hold the hook as you would a pencil, grasping it between your thumb and index finger, in the middle of the flat thumb rest. Your middle finger is positioned on the other side to balance the hook.

Knife grip

Hold the hook in the same manner as you would hold a knife, grasping it between your thumb on one side and index and middle finger on the other side, resting the end of the hook against your palm.

Hold the yarn

The free hand holds your crochetwork and at the same time controls the tension of the yarn. You can weave the yarn through your fingers or just place the thread between your palm and two or three fingers. Keep in mind that you have to maintain a steady tension while crocheting, so that your stitches come out even.

Tension

It can be challenging to master the tension of your yarn when you are new to crochet. You are not alone – tension is the one thing that most beginning crocheters have a hard time with.
To maintain tension in the working yarn, you may find it helpful to unravel a long end of your yarn ball (your tension is tighter when the weight of the ball pulls your yarn tight), and wrap the yarn around the fingers of the hand opposite the one holding the hook.

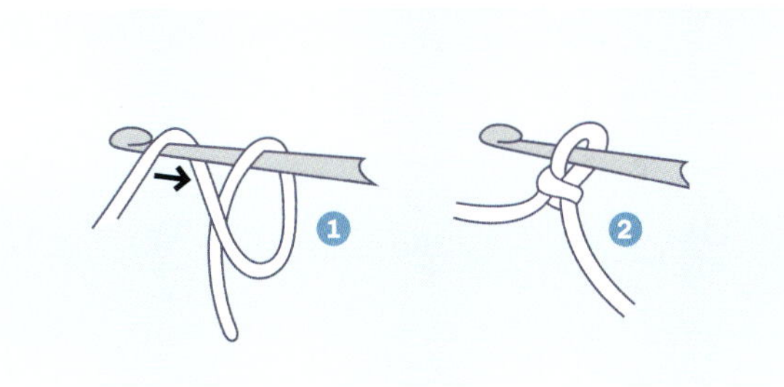

SLIP KNOT

Tying a slip knot onto the crochet hook is one of the first things you need to know to get started with crocheting. It's like casting the yarn onto the hook so you can start crocheting.

Step 1: Wrap the yarn into a loop, so that the shorter strand lies behind the longer one. Insert the crochet hook through the loop, catch the longer yarn and bring it through the loop.

Step 2: Pull on both ends of the yarn to tighten the knot around the hook.

Scan or visit **www.stitch.show/slipknot** for the video tutorial

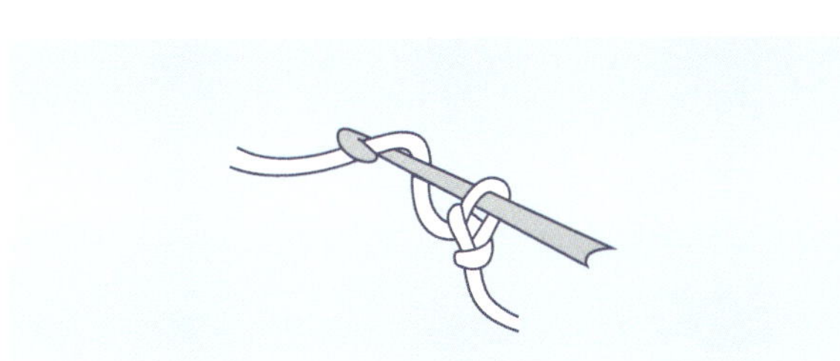

YARN OVER HOOK

The yarn over hook technique is used in every type of crochet stitch. Wrap the yarn over the hook from back to front. Now that he yarn is wrapped around the tip of the crochet hook, the hook can grab and pull the yarn.

Scan or visit **www.stitch.show/yoh** for the video tutorial

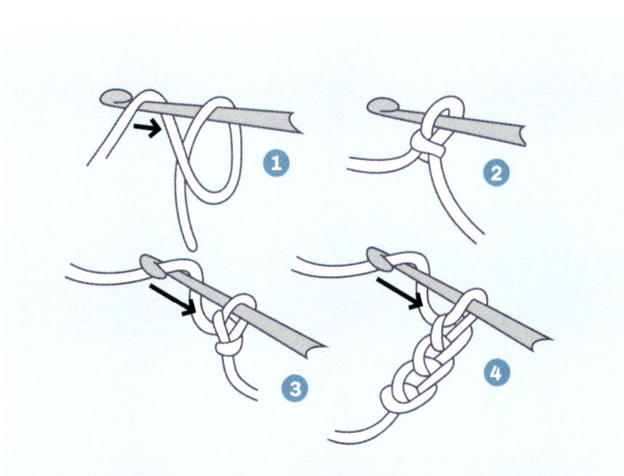

CHAIN *(abbreviation: ch)*

If you're working in rows, your first row will be a series of chain stitches.

Step 1: Use the hook to draw the yarn through the loop.

Step 2: Pull the loop until tight.

Step 3: Wrap the yarn over the hook from back to front. Pull the hook, carrying the yarn, through the loop already on your hook. You have now completed one chain stitch.

Step 4: Repeat these steps as indicated in the pattern to create a foundation chain.

Scan or visit **www.stitch.show/ch** for the video tutorial

INSERT THE HOOK (PLACEMENT OF STITCHES)

With the exception of chains, all crochet stitches require the hook to be inserted in existing stitches. Insert the hook underneath both top loops of the stitch in the row or round below. When inserting the hook, you take it from front to back through a stitch. The point of the hook must always look down or sideways, so the hook doesn't snag the yarn or the fabric.

When asked to crochet FLO or BLO you make the same stitch, but leave one loop untouched.

Inserting the hook in front loops only *(abbreviation: FLO)*

When working in Front Loops Only, you pick up only the front loop towards you.

Inserting the hook in back loops only *(abbreviation: BLO)*

When working in Back Loops Only, you pick up only the back loop away from you.

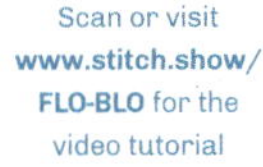

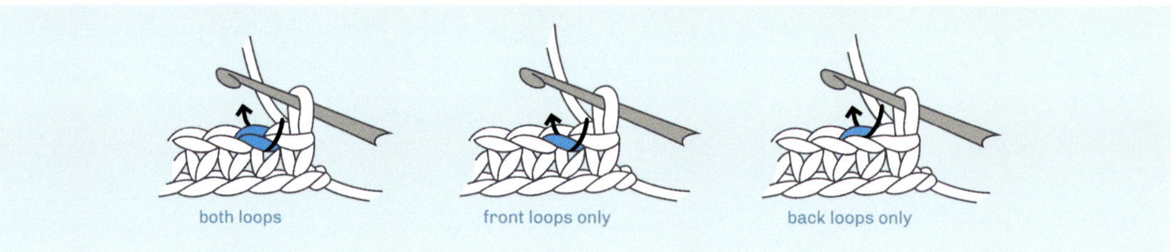

SINGLE CROCHET *(abbreviation: sc)*

Single crochet is the stitch that will be most frequently used in this book.

Step 1: Insert the hook into the next stitch.

Step 2: Wrap the yarn over the hook. Pull the yarn through the stitch. You will see that there are now two loops on the hook.

Step 3: Wrap the yarn over the hook again and draw it through both loops at once.

Step 4: You have now completed one single crochet.

Step 5: Insert the hook into the next stitch to continue.

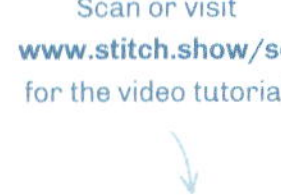

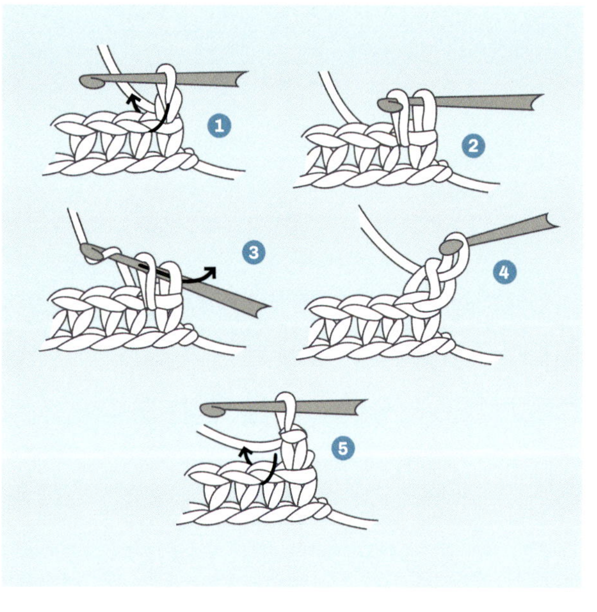

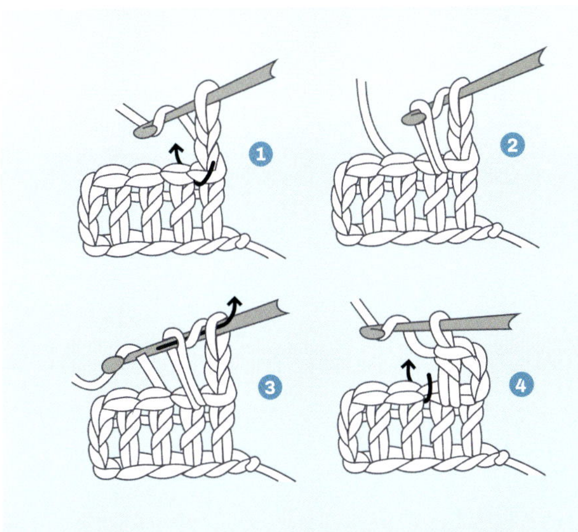

HALF DOUBLE CROCHET *(abbreviation: hdc)*

Step 1: Bring your yarn over the hook from back to front before placing the hook in the stitch.
Step 2: Wrap the yarn over the hook and draw the yarn through the stitch. You now have three loops on the hook.
Step 3: Wrap the yarn over the hook again and pull it through all three loops on the hook. You have completed your first half double crochet.
Step 4: To continue, bring your yarn over the hook and insert it in the next stitch.

Scan or visit **www.stitch.show/hdc** for the video tutorial

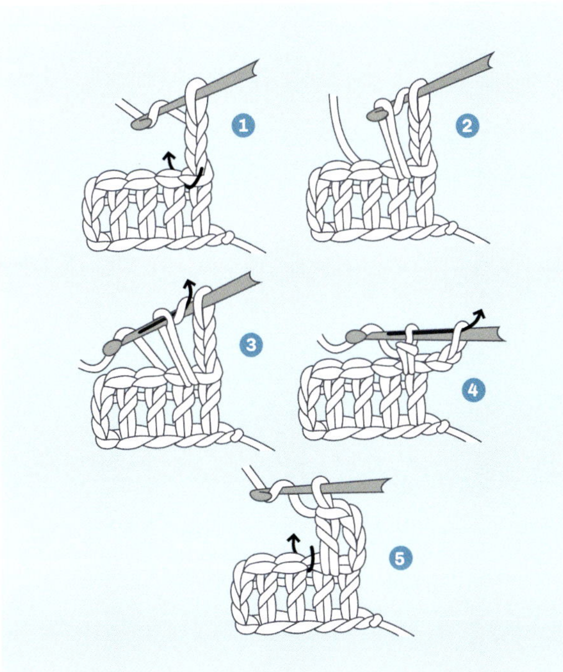

DOUBLE CROCHET *(abbreviation: dc)*

Step 1: Bring your yarn over the hook from back to front before placing the hook in the stitch.
Step 2: Wrap the yarn over the hook and draw the yarn through the stitch. You now have three loops on the hook.
Step 3: Wrap the yarn over the hook again and pull it through the first two loops on the hook. You now have two loops on the hook.
Step 4: Wrap the yarn over the hook one last time and draw it through both loops on the hook. You have now completed one double crochet.
Step 5: To continue, bring your yarn over the hook and insert it in the next stitch.

Scan or visit **www.stitch.show/dc** for the video tutorial

Scan or visit **www.stitch.show/slst** for the video tutorial

SLIP STITCH *(abbreviation: slst)*

A slip stitch is used to move across one or more stitches at once or to finish a piece.

Step 1: Insert your hook into the next stitch.

Step 2: Wrap the yarn over the hook and draw through the stitch and loop on your hook at once.

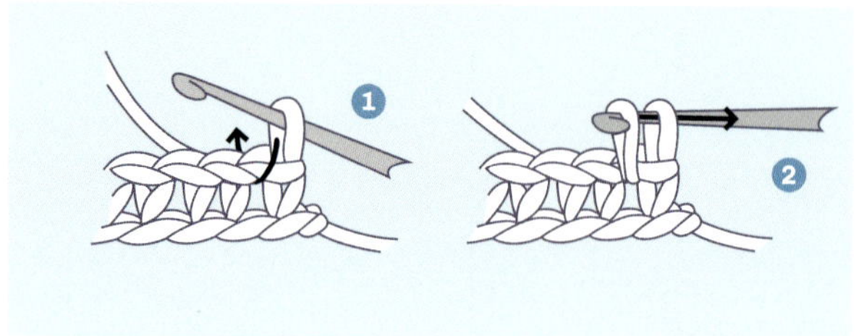

INVISIBLE DECREASE *(abbreviation: dec)*

When decreasing, two stitches are crocheted together. The number of stitches in a round therefore decreases and the piece shrinks.

Step 1: Insert the hook in the front loop of your first stitch. Now immediately insert your hook in the front loop of the second stitch. You now have three loops on your hook.

Step 2: Wrap the yarn over the hook and pull it through the first two loops on the hook.

Step 3: Wrap the yarn over the hook again and pull it through the remaining two loops on the hook. You have now completed one invisible decrease.

Scan or visit **www.stitch.show/dec** for the video tutorial

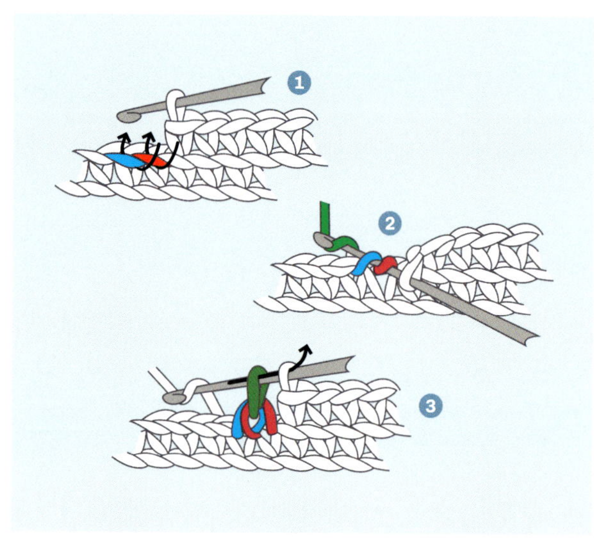

INCREASE *(abbreviation: inc)*

To increase, two single crochet stitches are made in the same stitch. This way, new stitches are created and the piece expands.

Step 1: Make a first single crochet stitch in the next stitch.

Step 2: Make a second single crochet stitch in the same stitch.

Scan or visit **www.stitch.show/inc** for the video tutorial

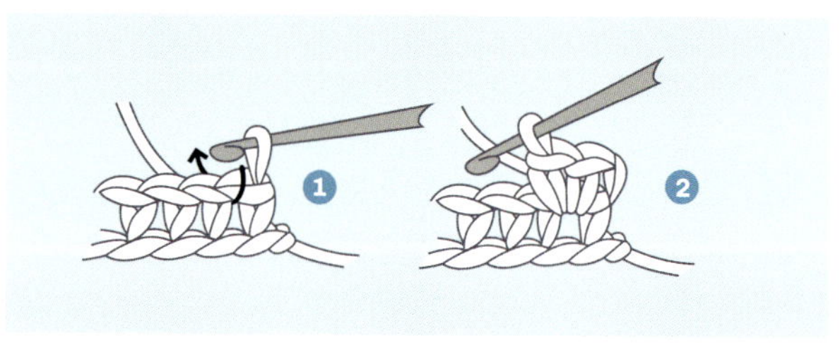

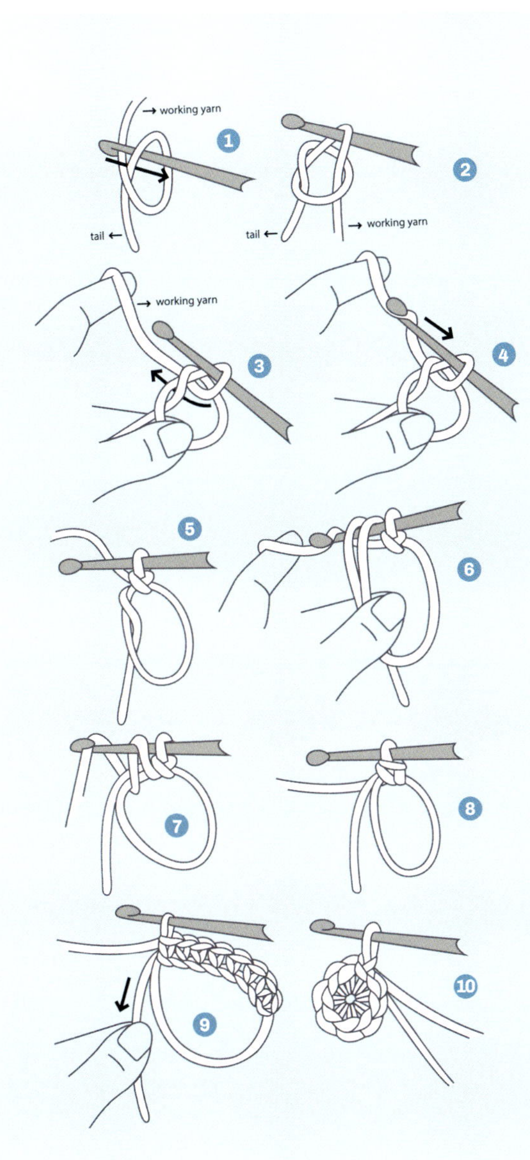

MAGIC RING

To start an amigurumi piece, you need a little circle. A magic ring is the ideal way to start crocheting in the round as there will be no hole left in the middle of your starting round. You start by crocheting over an adjustable loop and finally pull the loop tight when you have finished the required number of stitches.

Step 1: Start with the yarn crossed to form a circle.

Step 2: Draw up a loop with your hook, but don't pull it tight.

Step 3: Hold the circle with your index finger and thumb and wrap the working yarn over your middle finger.

Step 4-5: Make one chain stitch by wrapping the yarn over the hook and pulling it through the loop on the hook.

Step 6: Now insert your hook into the circle and underneath the tail. Wrap the yarn over the hook and draw up a loop.

Step 7: Keep your hook above the circle and wrap the yarn over the hook again.

Step 8: Pull it through both loops on the hook. You have now completed your first single crochet stitch.

Continue to crochet (repeating step 6, 7, 8) until you have the required number of stitches as mentioned in the pattern.

Step 9-10: Now grab the yarn tail and pull to draw the center of the ring tightly.

You can now begin your second round by crocheting into the first single crochet stitch of the magic ring. You can use a stitch marker to remember where you started.

Scan or visit **www.stitch.show/magicring** for the video tutorial

Challenging? You can try the alternative method.
Tutorial on the next page →

STARTING A CIRCULAR PIECE WITH TWO CHAIN STITCHES

If you don't want to use the magic ring technique, there's an easier way to start crocheting in the round. The downside of this technique is a tiny hole that remains visible in the center of the piece.

Scan or visit **www.stitch.show/2ch** for the video tutorial

Step 1: Start by making a slip knot. Then, make 2 chain stitches and work x sc into the second chain from the hook – where x is the number of sc stitches you would make in your magic ring.

Step 2: Make a slst in the first stitch. You now have a little circle to start with.

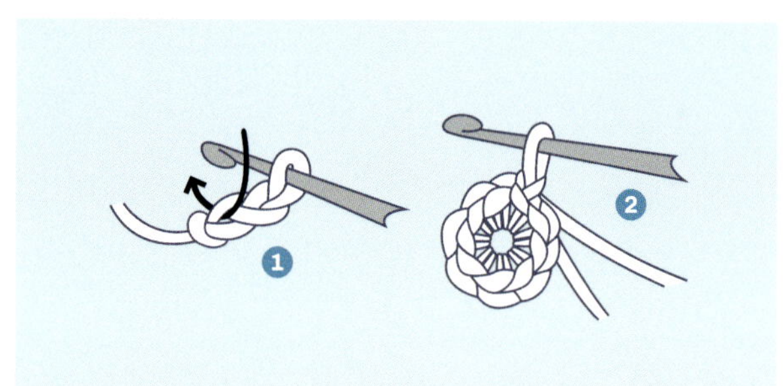

CROCHET AROUND A FOUNDATION CHAIN

Some pieces start with an oval. You make an oval by crocheting around a foundation chain.

Step 1: Crochet a foundation chain with as many chains as mentioned in the pattern and skip the first chain on the hook.

Step 2-3: Work a sc stitch in the next chain stitch. Work your crochet stitches into each chain across as mentioned in the pattern.

Step 4: The last stitch before turning is usually an increase stitch.

Step 5: Turn your work upside down to work into the underside of the chain stitches. You'll notice that only one loop is available, simply insert your hook in this loop. Work your stitches into each chain across.

Scan or visit **www.stitch.show/oval** for the video tutorial

Step 6: When finished, your last stitch should be next to the first stitch you made. You can now continue working in spirals.

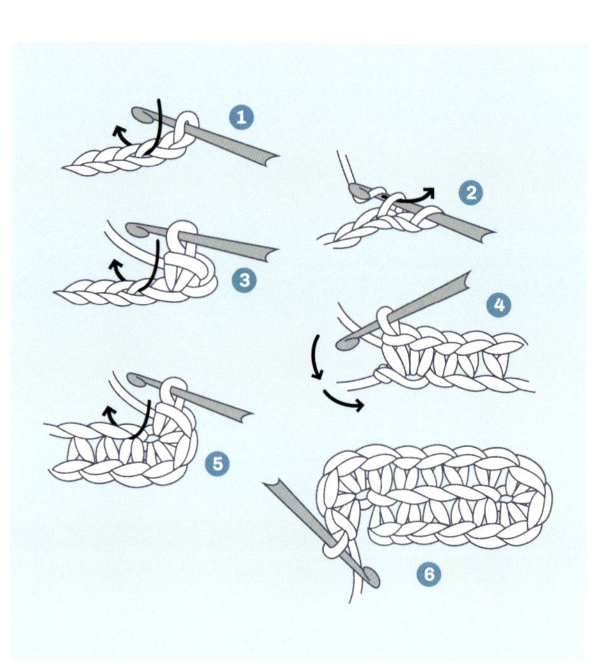

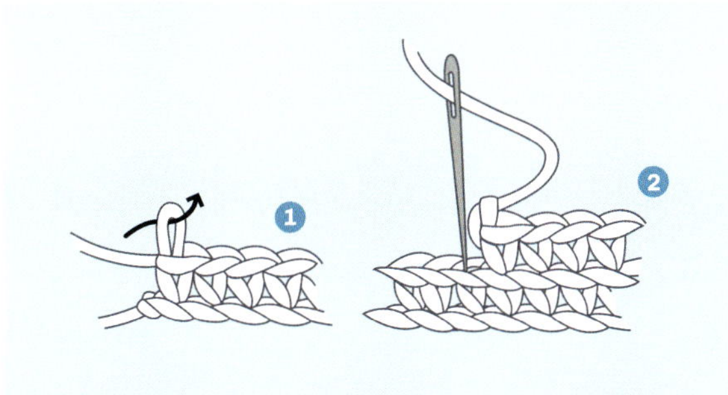

FASTENING OFF

Step 1: When you've finished crocheting, cut the yarn a couple of inches / cm from your last stitch. Pull the yarn through the last loop until it is all the way through. You now have a finished knot.

Step 2: Thread the long tail through a tapestry needle and insert it through the back loop of the next stitch. This way the finishing knot will remain invisible in your finished piece. You can use this yarn tail to continue sewing the pieces together.

Scan or visit **www.stitch.show/fastenoff** for the video tutorial

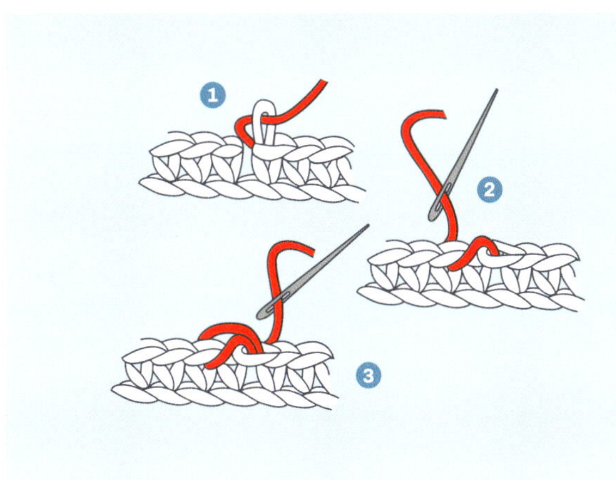

FASTENING OFF – INVISIBLE JOIN

Step 1: After completing the last stitch, cut your yarn, leaving a long yarn tail. Pull the yarn tail all the way through the stitch.

Step 2: Take the yarn tail on your tapestry needle. Insert your needle underneath both loops of the second stitch of the round, from front to back.

Step 3: Then insert it into the back loop only of the last stitch you made. Pull the tail to the back of the work and weave in the yarn end. You will see that your invisible join covers the first stitch of the round.

Scan or visit **www.stitch.show/fastenoff-invisible** for the video tutorial

INVISIBLE COLOR CHANGE

When you want to switch from one color to the next, you work to within two stitches before a color change.

Step 1: Make the next single crochet stitch as usual, but don't pull the final loop through.

Step 2-3: Instead, wrap the new color of yarn around your hook and pull it through the remaining loops.

To make a neat color change, you can make the first stitch in the new color a slip stitch instead of a single crochet. Don't pull the slip stitch too tight or it will be difficult to crochet into in the next round. Tie the loose tails in a knot and leave them on the inside.

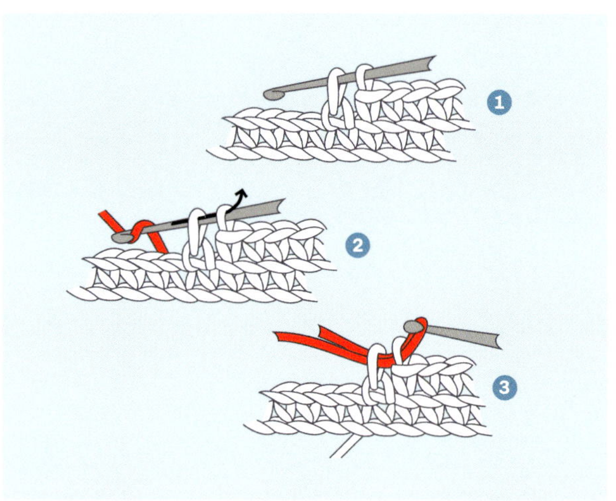

Scan or visit **www.stitch.show/colorchange** for the video tutorial

TIP: When changing color, I like to weave in the leftover yarn ends at the same time. I start by weaving in the new yarn color 3 to 4 stitches before I want to make the color change. Hold the new color of yarn behind your crochet work and crochet around it. When you reach the point where you want to make a color change, you change to the new color. I then hide the original color yarn tail by crocheting it along in the next 3 to 4 stitches.

TIP: If you're working several color changes in a round, you can opt for the tapestry technique, where you don't cut and tie the unused color each time, but instead carry it on the inside of your work until you need to use it next. Make sure that you let the unworked yarn hang loosely on the inside of your work, so it doesn't cinch everything together.

Excited to test your color-changing skills? This cow is perfect for experimenting!

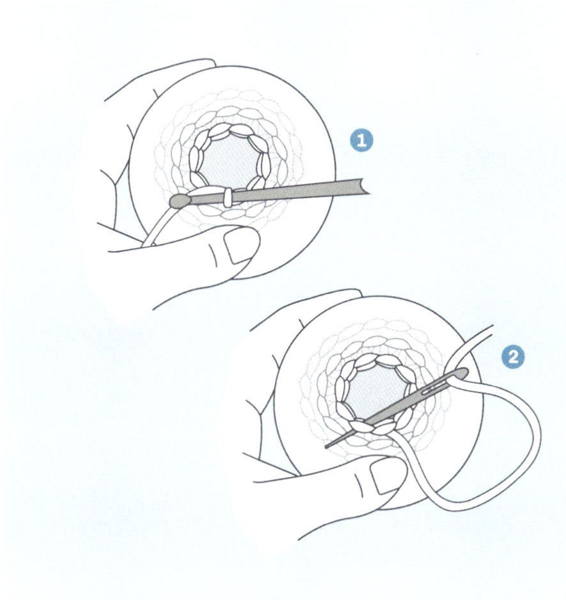

CLOSING OFF A PIECE

Step 1: After several decreases in the last round, a small hole will remain at the end of some pieces.

Step 2: Thread the yarn tail left at the end of the piece onto a yarn needle, then insert the needle through each of the front loops of the stitches in the last round. Tighten and insert the needle through the nearest stitch, make a knot, and hide the yarn tail inside the piece.

Scan or visit **www.stitch.show/closing** for the video tutorial

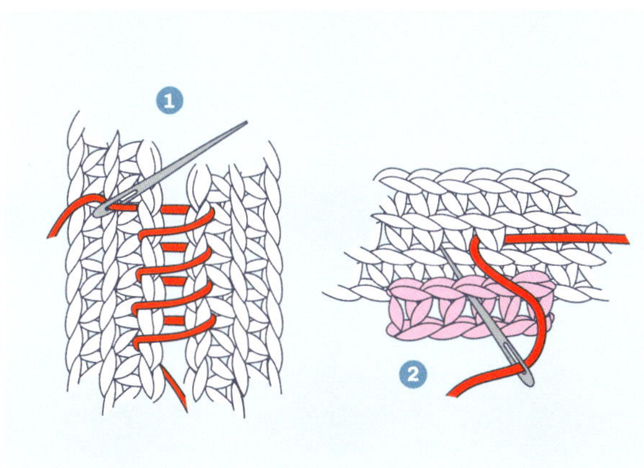

TIP: Always make sure the pieces are securely attached so that they can't be pulled off. Make small, neat stitches and try to make them show as little as possible.

JOINING PARTS – SEWING

First, pin the parts you want to sew to one another, so you can evaluate the result and adjust if necessary. If possible, use the leftover yarn tail from when you fastened off, or use a new length of the same yarn color of one of the pieces that you want to join.

Option 1 – When the different pieces are open: position the piece on the body and sew all around it, going through the stitches of both the extremity and the body.

Option 2 – When the opening of a piece is sewn closed before attaching: line up the stitches and sew through both loops of the open side and between the stitches of the closed side. Use the same color of yarn as the pieces you want to join together.

Scan or visit **www.stitch.show/joining-sewing** for the video tutorial

JOINING PARTS – CROCHETING PIECES TOGETHER

Two or more smaller pieces can be joined into one big piece (such as where two fins are joined to make the tail).

On the first piece, you fasten off and cut the yarn, leaving a tail of about 6" / 15 cm. On the second piece, you do not fasten off. Continue crocheting on the second piece. Crochet the required number of stitches on the second piece.

Scan or visit **www.stitch.show/joining-crocheting** for the video tutorial

Step 1-2: Then, pick up the first piece and insert your hook in the first stitch to the left of the last stitch made. Pull up a loop and crochet a single crochet stitch.

Step 3: Continue crocheting the required number of stitches around.

Step 4: Then, jump to the second piece again by inserting your hook in the first unused stitch and continue crocheting until the end of the round. You have now created a new, bigger round by bringing together two smaller rounds.

TIP: The small opening between the pieces can be sewn closed with the yarn tail from the first piece.

Materials
Sport weight yarn in
  Light gray (10 grams)
  Dark gray (leftover)
  Pink (leftover)
  Black (leftover)
B-1 / 2.5 mm crochet hook
Yarn needle
Pins
Scissors
Stitch markers
Fiberfill for stuffing

Size
2.8 inches / 7 cm tall when made with the indicated yarn

Skills needed
magic ring *(page 17)*

DO YOU WANT TO MAKE A CHENILLE CAT?

Materials:
Chenille super bulky weight yarn in
  Light gray (30 grams)
  Dark gray (6 grams)
  Pink (leftover)
  Black (leftover)
H-8 / 5 mm crochet hook

Size:
This will result in a 5" / 13 cm tall cat

Scan or visit **www.amigurumi.com/5401** to share pictures and find inspiration in our gallery.

LILY THE CAT

Lily the Cat is sharing an apartment with her roommate Oliver the Mouse. They make for a somewhat unlikely duo, but they actually have lots in common, such as a love for dairy products, long naps on the windowsill and nighttime mischief. When they get bored, they play hide-and-seek, tag or one of the many board games that fill their shelves. Life is good when you have a friend to share it with.

1

2

3

4

HEAD AND BODY *(in light gray yarn)*

Rnd 1: start 6 sc in a magic ring [6]
Rnd 2: inc in all 6 st [12]
Rnd 3: (sc in next st, inc in next st) repeat 6 times [18]
Rnd 4: (sc in next 2 st, inc in next st) repeat 6 times [24]
Rnd 5: sc in all 24 st [24]
Rnd 6: (sc in next 3 st, inc in next st) repeat 6 times [30]
Rnd 7: sc in all 30 st [30]
Rnd 8: (sc in next 9 st, inc in next st) repeat 3 times [33]
Mark the 14th and 19th stitch of round 8 with a stitch marker.
Rnd 9 – 10: sc in all 33 st [33]
Rnd 11: (sc in next 9 st, dec) repeat 3 times [30]
With black yarn, embroider the eyes over round 8, using the marked stitches as a guide ❶.
With pink yarn, embroider the nose between rounds 8 and 9, 1 stitch wide, centered between the eyes ❷. You count 2 stitches between each eye and the nose.
With dark gray yarn, embroider 3 long stripes on the top of the head, covering 4 rounds at the front and 3 rounds at the back ❸.
With dark gray yarn, embroider 4 stripes on the sides of the head, 2 on each side. The top stripes are positioned between rounds 8 and 9 and are each 4 stitches wide. The bottom stripes are positioned between rounds 9 and 10 and are each 6 stitches wide ❹.
Stuff the head with fiberfill and continue stuffing the head and body as you go.
Rnd 12: (sc in next 3 st, dec) repeat 6 times [24]
Rnd 13: (sc in next 2 st, dec) repeat 6 times [18]
Rnd 14: sc in all 18 st [18]
Rnd 15: (sc in next 2 st, inc in next st) repeat 6 times [24]
Rnd 16 – 18: sc in all 24 st [24]
With dark gray yarn, embroider 2 stripes on the back of the body, one stripe between rounds 15 and 16 (6 stitches wide) and one stripe between rounds 16 and 17 (4 stitches wide) ❺.
Rnd 19: (sc in next st, dec) repeat 8 times [16]
Rnd 20: dec 8 times [8]
Finish stuffing the head and body. Fasten off, leaving a yarn tail. Using your yarn needle, weave the yarn tail through the front loop of each remaining stitch and pull it tight to close. Weave in the yarn end.

5

6

7

EAR *(make 2, in light gray yarn)*

Rnd 1: start 4 sc in a magic ring [4]
Rnd 2: (sc in next st, inc in next st) repeat 2 times [6]
Rnd 3: (sc in next 2 st, inc in next st) repeat 2 times [8]
Rnd 4: (sc in next 3 st, inc in next st) repeat 2 times [10]

Slst in next st. Fasten off, leaving a long tail for sewing. The ears don't need to be stuffed. Flatten the ears and sew them between rounds 3 and 8 of the head, with an interspace of 6 stitches 6.

TAIL *(in light gray yarn)*

Rnd 1: start 6 sc in a magic ring [6]
Rnd 2: (sc in next st, inc in next st) repeat 3 times [9]
Rnd 3 – 4: sc in all 9 st [9]
Rnd 5: (sc in next st, dec) repeat 3 times [6]
Rnd 6 – 11: sc in all 6 st [6]

Stuff the tail lightly with fiberfill. Fasten off, leaving a yarn tail. Using your yarn needle, weave the yarn tail through the front loop of each remaining stitch and pull it tight to close. Sew rounds 6-11 of the tail to round 18 of the body, letting it curve around the back of the body 7.

FRONT LEG *(make 2, in light gray yarn)*

Rnd 1: start 6 sc in a magic ring [6]

Slst in next st. Fasten off, leaving a long tail for sewing. Sew the legs right next to each other to the front of the body, between rounds 17-20.

Materials
Sport weight yarn in
Pistachio green (6 grams)
Amazon green (4 grams)
Emerald green (leftover)
Beryl green (leftover)
B-1 / 2.5 mm crochet hook
Safety eyes (8 mm)
Yarn needle
Pins
Scissors
Stitch markers
Fiberfill for stuffing

Size
3.5" / 9 cm long when made with the indicated yarn

Skills needed
magic ring *(page 17)*
changing color *(page 20)*

DO YOU WANT TO MAKE A CHENILLE CATERPILLAR?

Materials:
Chenille super bulky weight yarn in
Pistachio green (18 grams)
Amazon green (12 grams)
Emerald green (9 grams)
Beryl green (9 grams)
H-8 / 5 mm crochet hook
Safety eyes (18 mm)

Size:
This will result in a 6.3" / 16 cm long caterpillar

Scan or visit **www.amigurumi.com/5402** to share pictures and find inspiration in our gallery.

CARLO THE CATERPILLAR

Carlo the Caterpillar is an apple aficionado. He has an extensive knowledge of the local orchards and he spends his days wriggling from one tree to another, closely inspecting and savoring as many fruits as he can. In addition, he can tell tens of different apple varieties apart. If you want to make a special apple platter for a party or a one-of-a-kind cider, Carlo is the caterpillar you need.

1

BODY *(start in amazon green yarn)*

Rnd 1: start 6 sc in a magic ring [6]
Rnd 2: inc in all 6 st [12]
Rnd 3: (sc in next st, inc in next st) repeat 6 times [18]
Rnd 4 – 6: sc in all 18 st [18]
Rnd 7: (sc in next st, dec) repeat 6 times [12]
Rnd 8: (sc in next st, dec) repeat 4 times [8]
Change to emerald green yarn.
Rnd 9: (sc in next st, inc in next st) repeat 4 times [12]
Stuff the body with fiberfill and continue stuffing as you go.
Rnd 10: (sc in next st, inc in next st) repeat 6 times [18]
Rnd 11 – 13: sc in all 18 st [18]
Rnd 14: (sc in next st, dec) repeat 6 times [12]
Rnd 15: (sc in next st, dec) repeat 4 times [8]
Change to beryl green yarn.
Rnd 16: (sc in next st, inc in next st) repeat 4 times [12]
Rnd 17: (sc in next st, inc in next st) repeat 6 times [18]
Rnd 18 – 20: sc in all 18 st [18]
Rnd 21: (sc in next st, dec) repeat 6 times [12]
Rnd 22: dec 6 times [6]
Fasten off, leaving a yarn tail. Using your yarn needle, weave the yarn tail through the front loop of each remaining stitch and pull it tight to close. Weave in the yarn end.

HEAD *(in pistachio green yarn)*

Rnd 1: start 6 sc in a magic ring [6]
Rnd 2: inc in all 6 st [12]
Rnd 3: (sc in next st, inc in next st) repeat 6 times [18]
Rnd 4: (sc in next 2 st, inc in next st) repeat 6 times [24]
Rnd 5: (sc in next 3 st, inc in next st) repeat 6 times [30]
Rnd 6 – 10: sc in all 30 st [30]
Insert the safety eyes between rounds 7 and 8, with an interspace of 6 stitches.
Rnd 11: (sc in next 3 st, dec) repeat 6 times [24]

Rnd 12: (sc in next 2 st, dec) repeat 6 times [18]
Rnd 13: (sc in next st, dec) repeat 6 times [12]
Slst in next st. Fasten off, leaving a long tail for sewing. Stuff the head with fiberfill. Sew the head between rounds 3 and 7 of the body ❶.

LEG *(make 6, in pistachio green yarn)*

Rnd 1: start 4 sc in a magic ring [4]
Slst in next st. Fasten off, leaving a long tail for sewing. Sew 2 legs at the bottom of each body part, with an interspace of 3 stitches across the belly. Sew the first pair of legs on rounds 3-5, the second pair of legs on rounds 11-13 and the third pair of legs on rounds 19-21.

ANTENNA *(make 2, in amazon green yarn)*

Rnd 1: start 6 sc in a magic ring [6]
Rnd 2 – 3: sc in all 6 st [6]
Rnd 4: (sc in next st, dec) repeat 2 times [4]
Slst in next st. Fasten off, leaving a long tail for sewing. You can put some stuffing in the antenna, but stuffing is optional. Sew the antennae on top of the head, on round 3, with an interspace of 4 stitches.

Materials
Sport weight yarn in
White (8 grams)
Yellow (leftover)
Red (leftover)
Black (leftover)
B-1 / 2.5 mm crochet hook
Yarn needle
Pins
Scissors
Stitch markers
Fiberfill for stuffing

Size
2" / 5 cm tall when made with the indicated yarn

Skills needed
magic ring *(page 17)*
half double crochet *(page 15)*
double crochet *(page 15)*
crocheting in rows *(page 11)*
fastening off invisible join *(page 19)*

DO YOU WANT TO MAKE A CHENILLE CHICKEN?

Materials:
Chenille super bulky weight yarn in
White (24 grams)
Yellow (leftover)
Red (6 grams)
Black (leftover)
H-8 / 5 mm crochet hook

Size:
This will result in a 4.7" / 12 cm tall chicken

Scan or visit **www.amigurumi.com/5403** to share pictures and find inspiration in our gallery.

ROSIE THE CHICKEN

Rosie has a way with words. If another farm animal comes round looking for a funny birthday wish, an inspirational quote to put up on the barn wall or a moving speech to toast to a loved one, Rosie is ready to help, and she'll craft the most beautiful texts. One of her friends suggested she turn her talent into a job, but Rosie declined, saying that it was her way of nurturing friendships.

HEAD AND BODY *(in white yarn)*

Rnd 1: start 6 sc in a magic ring [6]
Rnd 2: inc in all 6 st [12]
Rnd 3: (sc in next 3 st, inc in next st) repeat 3 times [15]
Rnd 4 – 5: sc in all 15 st [15]
Mark the 5th and 10th stitch of round 5 with a stitch marker.
Rnd 6: (sc in next 4 st, inc in next st) repeat 3 times [18]
In the next round, we'll make chains to create the 'spine' of the chicken's back.
Rnd 7: slst in next st, ch 4 ①, start in second ch from hook, sc in next 3 ch ②, sc in same st on the body where you made the slst ③, sc in next 17 st on the body [21] ④ ⑤
Rnd 8: sc in the other side of next 3 ch, inc in next st, sc in next 5 st, inc in next st, sc in next 2 st, inc in next st, sc in next st, inc in next st, sc in next st, inc in next st, sc in next 2 st, inc in next st, sc in next 4 st [30] ⑥
Rnd 9 – 11: sc in all 30 st [30]
Rnd 12: sc in next st, dec 3 times, sc in next 4 st, dec, sc in next 2 st, dec, (sc in next st, dec) repeat 2 times, sc in next 2 st, dec, sc in next st, dec [21]
Rnd 13: dec, sc in next st, dec 2 times, sc in next 14 st [18]
With black yarn, embroider the eyes on round 5, using the marked stitches as a guide.
Rnd 14: (sc in next st, dec) repeat 6 times [12]
Stuff the head and body with fiberfill and continue stuffing as you go.
Rnd 15: dec 6 times [6]
Fasten off, leaving a yarn tail. Using your yarn needle, weave the yarn tail through the front loop of each remaining stitch and pull it tight to close. Weave in the yarn end.

BEAK *(in yellow yarn)*

Rnd 1: start 6 sc in a magic ring [6]
Fasten off with an invisible join, leaving a long tail for sewing. Sew the beak on rounds 5 and 6 of the head, centered between the eyes.

COMB PART 1 *(in red yarn)*

Rnd 1: start 7 sc in a magic ring [7]
Rnd 2: sc in all 7 st [7]
Slst in next st. Fasten off, leaving a long tail for sewing.

COMB PART 2 *(in red yarn)*

Rnd 1: start 5 sc in a magic ring [5]
Rnd 2: sc in all 5 st [5]
Slst in next st. Fasten off, leaving a long tail for sewing. Sew comb part 1 between rounds 1 and 2 at the front of the head. Sew comb part 2 between rounds 1 and 2 at the back of the head.

WING *(make 2, in white yarn)*

Rnd 1: start 6 sc in a magic ring [6]
Rnd 2: inc in next 2 st, hdc + dc + hdc in next st, inc in next 3 st [13]
Fasten off with an invisible join, leaving a long tail for sewing. Sew the wings on the sides of the body, at an angle, with the top of the wings on round 7 and the bottom of the wings on round 11. The tip of the wings is pointing towards the back of the body. Sew all around the wings.

Materials
Sport weight yarn in
Red (15 grams)
B-1 / 2.5 mm crochet hook
Safety eyes (7 mm)
Yarn needle
Pins
Scissors
Stitch markers
Fiberfill for stuffing

Size
4.3" / 11 cm wide when made with the indicated yarn

Skills needed
magic ring *(page 17)*
crocheting in front and back loops only *(page 14)*
joining parts – crocheting pieces together *(page 22)*
fastening off invisible join *(page 19)*

DO YOU WANT TO MAKE A CHENILLE CRAB?

Materials:
Chenille super bulky weight yarn in
Red (45 grams)
H-8 / 5 mm crochet hook
Safety eyes (15 mm)

Size:
This will result in a 6.7" / 17 cm wide crab

Scan or visit **www.amigurumi.com/5404** to share pictures and find inspiration in our gallery.

SNAPPY THE CRAB

Snappy the Crab prefers solitude over the bustling sounds of the tide. While his crab friends hurry over the shore, chattering about this and that, Snappy hides himself between the rocks and looks for colorful pebbles. One day, a shy little octopus joined him, and without saying much, they found a quiet companionship in their shared love of peaceful moments.

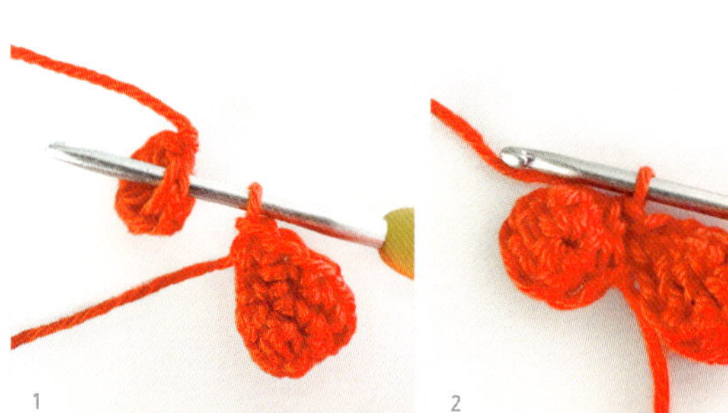

CLAW *(make 2)*

Start by making 2 claw parts.

Small part *(in red yarn)*

Rnd 1: start 4 sc in a magic ring [4]
Rnd 2: (sc in next st, inc in next st) repeat 2 times [6]
Slst in next st. Fasten off and weave in the yarn end.

Big part *(in red yarn)*

Rnd 1: start 4 sc in a magic ring [4]
Rnd 2: (sc in next st, inc in next st) repeat 2 times [6]
Rnd 3: (sc in next 2 st, inc in next st) repeat 2 times [8]

In the next round we'll join the claw parts together to create the claw.
Rnd 4: sc in next 4 st on the big part, continue in the first st of the small part ❶, sc in all 6 st on the small part ❷ ❸, continue in the fifth st of the big part, sc in next 4 st on the big part [14] ❹
Rnd 5 – 6: sc in all 14 st [14]
Rnd 7: (sc in next 5 st, dec) repeat 2 times [12]
Stuff the claw lightly with fiberfill and continue stuffing as you go.
Rnd 8: dec 6 times [6]
Rnd 9 – 11: sc in all 6 st [6]
Slst in next st. Fasten off, leaving a yarn tail.

LEG *(make 6, in red yarn)*

Rnd 1: start 4 sc in a magic ring [4]
Rnd 2: (sc in next st, inc in next st) repeat 2 times [6]
Rnd 3 – 5: sc in all 6 st [6]
Slst in next st. Fasten off and weave in the yarn end. The legs don't need to be stuffed.

BODY *(in red yarn)*

Rnd 1: start 8 sc in a magic ring [8]
Rnd 2: inc in all 8 st [16]
Rnd 3: (sc in next st, inc in next st) repeat 8 times [24]
Rnd 4: sc in all 24 st [24]
Rnd 5: (sc in next 3 st, inc in next st) repeat 6 times [30]
Rnd 6: sc in all 30 st [30]
Rnd 7: (sc in next 4 st, inc in next st) repeat 6 times [36]
Rnd 8: BLO sc in all 36 st [36]

In the next round, we'll join the legs and claws to the body. Flatten the leg or claw and hold it next to the body, on the outside. To attach them, you work the next stitches through both layers of the leg/claw and the body (so working through 3 layers at once). Hide the yarn tails of the legs/claws inside the body.

Rnd 9: sc in next 4 st, (work through both a flattened leg and the body: sc in next 3 st) repeat 3 times ⑤ ⑥, work through both a flattened claw and the body: sc in next 3 st, continue working on the body, sc in next 8 st, work through both a flattened claw and the body: sc in next 3 st, (work through both a flattened leg and the body: sc in next 3 st) repeat 3 times [36]

Rnd 10: (sc in next 4 st, dec) repeat 6 times [30]

Insert the safety eyes between rounds 6 and 7, with an interspace of 5 stitches.

Rnd 11: (sc in next 3 st, dec) repeat 6 times [24]

Stuff the body with fiberfill and continue stuffing as you go.

Rnd 12: (sc in next st, dec) repeat 8 times [16]

Rnd 13: dec 8 times [8]

Fasten off, leaving a yarn tail. Using your yarn needle, weave the yarn tail through the front loop of each remaining stitch and pull it tight to close. Weave in the yarn end.

SHELL BORDER *(in red yarn)*

Pull up a loop of red yarn in the last leftover front loop of round 8 ⑦. Work the first stitch of the first round in the next front loop.

Rnd 1: FLO (sc in next 5 st, inc in next st) repeat 6 times [42] ⑧

Rnd 2: sc in all 42 st [42]

Fasten off with an invisible join and weave in the yarn end.

Materials
Sport weight yarn in
- Beige (10 grams)
- Brown (leftover)
- Dark brown (leftover)
- Black (leftover)

B-1 / 2.5 mm crochet hook
Yarn needle
Pins
Scissors
Stitch markers
Fiberfill for stuffing

Size
2.4" / 6 cm tall when made with the indicated yarn

Skills needed
magic ring *(page 17)*

DO YOU WANT TO MAKE A CHENILLE DOG?

Materials:
Chenille super bulky weight yarn in
- Beige (30 grams)
- Brown (9 grams)
- Dark brown (leftover)
- Black (leftover)

H-8 / 5 mm crochet hook

Size:
This will result in a 6" / 15 cm tall dog

Scan or visit **www.amigurumi.com/5405** to share pictures and find inspiration in our gallery.

LEX THE DOG

Lex the Dog has a passion for running. Every morning, as the sun peeks over the hills, Lex races out of his house, over the lawn, across the street and into the nearest woodland. He'll chase shadows and rays of sunshine, little birds and tiny squirrels, excitedly barking 'hello' to every critter and tree. Running makes Lex feel alive and free!

HEAD AND BODY *(in beige yarn)*

Rnd 1: start 6 sc in a magic ring [6]
Rnd 2: inc in all 6 st [12]
Rnd 3: (sc in next st, inc in next st) repeat 6 times [18]
Rnd 4: (sc in next 2 st, inc in next st) repeat 6 times [24]
Rnd 5: sc in all 24 st [24]
Rnd 6: (sc in next 3 st, inc in next st) repeat 6 times [30]
Rnd 7: sc in all 30 st [30]
Rnd 8: (sc in next 4 st, inc in next st) repeat 6 times [36]
Rnd 9 – 11: sc in all 36 st [36]
Rnd 12: (sc in next 4 st, dec) repeat 6 times [30]

With black yarn, embroider the eyes over round 8, with an interspace of 9 stitches ❶. With dark brown yarn, embroider a vertical stripe over 2 rounds below the spot where you want to position the nose. Next, embroider the nose over rounds 8-9 between the eyes, making it 3 stitches wide ❷ ❸.

Rnd 13: (sc in next 3 st, dec) repeat 6 times [24]
Rnd 14: (sc in next st, dec) repeat 8 times [16]
Rnd 15: sc in all 16 st [16]
Rnd 16: (sc in next st, inc in next st) repeat 8 times [24]

Stuff the head and body with fiberfill and continue stuffing as you go.

Rnd 17 – 19: sc in all 24 st [24]
Rnd 20: (sc in next st, dec) repeat 8 times [16]
Rnd 21: dec 8 times [8]

Fasten off, leaving a yarn tail. Using your yarn needle, weave the yarn tail through the front loop of each remaining stitch and pull it tight to close. Weave in the yarn end.

EAR *(make 2, in brown yarn)*

Rnd 1: start 6 sc in a magic ring [6]
Rnd 2: (sc in next st, inc in next st) repeat 3 times [9]
Rnd 3 – 5: sc in all 9 st [9]
Rnd 6: (sc in next st, dec) repeat 3 times [6]
Rnd 7 – 8: sc in all 6 st [6]
Fasten off, leaving a yarn tail. The ears don't need to be stuffed. Using your yarn needle, weave the yarn tail through the front loop of each remaining stitch and pull it tight to close. Flatten the ears and place them on each side of the head, starting at round 6. Sew the top part of each ear to rounds 6-8 ❹, leaving the lower part unsewn so it hangs freely.

LEG *(make 2, in beige yarn)*

Rnd 1: start 6 sc in a magic ring [6]
Fasten off, leaving a long tail for sewing. Sew the legs on round 19 of the body, with an interspace of 1 stitch.

TAIL *(in beige yarn)*

Rnd 1: start 6 sc in a magic ring [6]
Rnd 2 – 9: sc in all 6 st [6]
Stuff the tail lightly with fiberfill. Fasten off, leaving a yarn tail. Using your yarn needle, weave the yarn tail through the front loop of each remaining stitch and pull it tight to close. Sew rounds 5-9 of the tail to round 17 of the body, letting it curve around the back of the body ❺ ❻.

Materials
Sport weight yarn in
Green (8 grams)
Light green (6 grams)
Yellow (8 grams)
B-1 / 2.5 mm crochet hook
Safety eyes (7 mm)
Yarn needle
Pins
Scissors
Stitch markers
Fiberfill for stuffing

Size
3" / 8 cm tall when made with the indicated yarn

Skills needed
magic ring *(page 17)*
changing color *(page 20)*

DO YOU WANT TO MAKE A CHENILLE DRAGONFLY?

Materials:
Chenille super bulky weight yarn in
Green (24 grams)
Light green (18 grams)
Yellow (24 grams)
H-8 / 5 mm crochet hook
Safety eyes (15 mm)

Size:
This will result in a 7.5" / 19 cm tall dragonfly

Scan or visit **www.amigurumi.com/5406** to share pictures and find inspiration in our gallery.

DAMON THE DRAGONFLY

Meet Damon the Dragonfly. He's a wise little insect and likes to chat with all kinds of animals visiting the pond. Once, he talked about swimming techniques with a cheerful cow and another time, a happy dog told him all about his favorite treats. Damon imparts his own stories and advice as well, telling everyone who visits him how time always moves forward, and to make the most of every day.

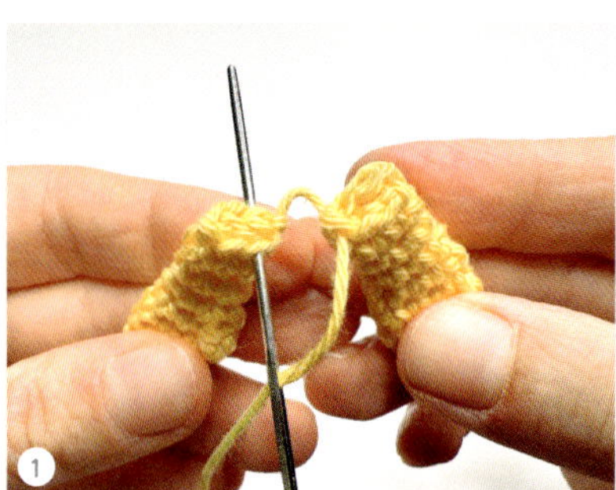

HEAD AND BODY *(start in green yarn)*

Rnd 1: start 8 sc in a magic ring [8]
Rnd 2: inc in all 8 st [16]
Rnd 3: (sc in next st, inc in next st) repeat 8 times [24]
Rnd 4: sc in all 24 st [24]
Rnd 5: (sc in next 3 st, inc in next st) repeat 6 times [30]
Rnd 6 – 9: sc in all 30 st [30]
Rnd 10: (sc in next 3 st, dec) repeat 6 times [24]
Insert the safety eyes between rounds 7 and 8, with an interspace of 5 stitches.
Rnd 11: (sc in next st, dec) repeat 8 times [16]
Stuff the head with fiberfill and continue stuffing the head and body as you go.
Rnd 12: dec 8 times [8]
Change to light green yarn.
Rnd 13: inc in all 8 st [16]
Rnd 14: (sc in next 7 st, inc in next st) repeat 2 times [18]
Rnd 15 – 16: sc in all 18 st [18]
Rnd 17: (sc in next st, dec) repeat 6 times [12]
Rnd 18: dec 6 times [6]
Change to green yarn.
Rnd 19 – 22: sc in all 6 st [6]
Fasten off, leaving a yarn tail. Using your yarn needle, weave the yarn tail through the front loop of each remaining stitch and pull it tight to close. Weave in the yarn end.

Rnd 7: (sc in next 2 st, dec) repeat 2 times [6]
Rnd 8 – 10: sc in all 6 st [6]
Slst in next st. Fasten off, leaving a long tail for sewing on the first top wing. Weave in the yarn end on the second top wing. The wings don't need to be stuffed. Flatten the wings. Hold both wings with the last rounds touching each other, and sew them together ❶ ❷ ❸.

ANTENNA *(make 2, in green yarn)*

Rnd 1: start 6 sc in a magic ring [6]
Rnd 2: sc in all 6 st [6]
Rnd 3: (sc in next st, dec) repeat 2 times [4]
Rnd 4: sc in all 4 st [4]
Slst in next st. Fasten off, leaving a long tail for sewing. You can stuff the antenna lightly, but stuffing is optional. Sew the antennae on round 3 of the head, with an interspace of 4 stitches.

TOP WING *(make 2, in yellow yarn)*

Rnd 1: start 6 sc in a magic ring [6]
Rnd 2: (sc in next 2 st, inc in next st) repeat 2 times [8]
Rnd 3 – 6: sc in all 8 st [8]

BOTTOM WING *(make 2, in yellow yarn)*

Rnd 1: start 6 sc in a magic ring [6]
Rnd 2: (sc in next 2 st, inc in next st) repeat 2 times [8]
Rnd 3 – 5: sc in all 8 st [8]
Rnd 6: (sc in next 2 st, dec) repeat 2 times [6]
Rnd 7 – 8: sc in all 6 st [6]
Slst in next st. Fasten off, leaving a long tail for sewing on the first bottom wing. Weave in the yarn end on the second bottom wing. The wings don't need to be stuffed. Flatten the wings. Hold both wings with the last rounds touching each other, and sew them together. Put the top wings on the bottom wings. Sew them together in the middle, over 6 rounds. Then sew the joined wings to the back of the body, over rounds 12-14.

Materials
Sport weight yarn in
- Green (5 grams)
- Brown (5 grams)
- White (leftover)
- Yellow (leftover)
- Orange (leftover)

B-1 / 2.5 mm crochet hook
Safety eyes (7 mm)
Yarn needle
Pins
Scissors
Stitch markers
Fiberfill for stuffing

Size
2.4" / 6 cm tall when made with the indicated yarn

Skills needed
magic ring *(page 17)*
changing color *(page 20)*
crocheting in rows *(page 11)*

DO YOU WANT TO MAKE A CHENILLE DUCK?

Materials:
Chenille super bulky weight yarn in
- Green (15 grams)
- Brown (15 grams)
- White (leftover)
- Yellow (leftover)
- Orange (6 grams)

H-8 / 5 mm crochet hook
Safety eyes (15 mm)

Size:
This will result in a 5" / 13 cm tall duck

Scan or visit **www.amigurumi.com/5407** to share pictures and find inspiration in our gallery.

MR. & MRS. DUCK

Mr. and Mrs. Duck live in a cosy little house by the river, the windows framed with flowers. Each morning, they waddle down to the water together, greeting their frog and fish neighbors on their way. While Mr. Duck fishes, Mrs. Duck tends to her waterside garden. And at dusk, they like to watch the fireflies dance, feeling deeply grateful for their calm and quiet life together.

Note: The color instructions in the pattern are for Mr. Duck. To make Mrs. Duck, simply crochet the head, body, and wings using white yarn.

HEAD AND BODY *(start in green yarn)*

Rnd 1: start 8 sc in a magic ring [8]
Rnd 2: inc in all 8 st [16]
Rnd 3: (sc in next st, inc in next st) repeat 8 times [24]
Rnd 4: (sc in next 3 st, inc in next st) repeat 6 times [30]
Rnd 5: sc in all 30 st [30]
Rnd 6: (sc in next 4 st, inc in next st) repeat 6 times [36]
Rnd 7 – 8: sc in all 36 st [36]
Mark the 12th and 19th stitch of round 8 with a stitch marker.
Rnd 9: sc in all 36 st [36]
Rnd 10: (sc in next 4 st, dec) repeat 6 times [30]
Rnd 11: (sc in next 3 st, dec) repeat 6 times [24]
Insert the safety eyes between rounds 8 and 9, in the stitches you marked earlier.
Rnd 12: (sc in next st, dec) repeat 8 times [16]
Change to white yarn 1 2 3 4.
Rnd 13: sc in all 16 st [16]
Change to brown yarn. In the next round, we'll make chains to create the 'spine' of the duck's back.
Rnd 14: slst in next st 5, ch 4 6, start in second ch from hook, sc in next 3 ch, continue in same st on the body where you made the slst 7, (sc in next 3 st, inc in next st) repeat 4 times [23] 8
Rnd 15: sc in the other side of next 3 ch, inc in next st, sc in next 22 st [27] 9
Stuff the head and body with fiberfill and continue stuffing as you go.
Rnd 16 – 17: sc in all 27 st [27]
Rnd 18: sc in next st, dec 3 times, sc in next st, (sc in next st, dec) repeat 6 times, sc in next st [18]
Rnd 19: dec, sc in next st, dec, sc in next 13 st [16]
Rnd 20: dec 8 times [8]
Fasten off, leaving a yarn tail. Using your yarn needle, weave the yarn tail through the front loop of each remaining stitch and pull it tight to close. Weave in the yarn end.

BEAK *(in yellow yarn)*

Rnd 1: start 6 sc in a magic ring [6]

Rnd 2: (sc in next 2 st, inc in next st) repeat 2 times [8]

Slst in next st. Fasten off, leaving a long tail for sewing. Flatten the beak and sew it to round 9 of the head, centered between the eyes.

FOOT *(make 2, in orange yarn)*

Rnd 1: start 6 sc in a magic ring [6]

Slst in next st. Fasten off, leaving a long tail for sewing. Sew the feet on rounds 19 and 20 of the body, with an interspace of 1 stitch ⑩.

WING *(make 2, in brown yarn)*

Rnd 1: start 6 sc in a magic ring [6]
Rnd 2 – 3: sc in all 6 st [6]
Rnd 4: (sc in next st, dec) repeat 2 times [4]

Slst in next st. Fasten off, leaving a yarn tail. The wings don't need to be stuffed. Using your yarn needle, weave the yarn tail through the front loop of each remaining stitch and pull it tight to close. Sew the wings on the sides of the body, at an angle, with the top of the wings on round 15 and the bottom of the wings on round 18. The tip of the wings is pointing towards the back of the body. Sew all around the wings, but leave the tip unsewn ⑪.

Materials
Sport weight yarn in
Yellow (7 grams)
Blue (5 grams)
B-1 / 2.5 mm crochet hook
Safety eyes (8 mm)
Yarn needle
Pins
Scissors
Stitch markers
Fiberfill for stuffing

Size
2.4" / 6 cm tall when made with the indicated yarn

Skills needed
magic ring *(page 17)*
changing color *(page 20)*

DO YOU WANT TO MAKE A CHENILLE ANGELFISH?

Materials:
Chenille super bulky weight yarn in
Yellow (21 grams)
Blue (15 grams)
H-8 / 5 mm crochet hook
Safety eyes (16 mm)

Size:
This will result in a 5.5" / 14 cm tall fish

Scan or visit **www.amigurumi.com/5408** to share pictures and find inspiration in our gallery.

LUNA THE ANGELFISH

Luna the Angelfish used to swim quietly through the coral reef, enjoying the sound of waves passing overhead. One day, a scuba diver accidentally dropped a water-proof speaker, and it sank all the way to the ocean floor. The music made her flutter her fins to the beat and twirl with joy. Before long, her fish friends joined in, turning the reef into a lively underwater dance hall.

HEAD AND BODY *(start in yellow yarn)*

Rnd 1: start 6 sc in a magic ring [6]
Rnd 2: (sc in next 2 st, inc in next st) repeat 2 times [8]
Rnd 3: sc in all 8 st [8]
Rnd 4: inc in all 8 st [16]
Rnd 5: (sc in next st, inc in next st) repeat 8 times [24]
Mark the 7th and 16th stitch of round 5 with a stitch marker.
Rnd 6: sc in all 24 st [24]
Note: *In the next few rounds, we'll make the color changes on the body. Instead of starting the color change in the last stitch of the previous round (as we normally would), these color changes start in the stitch before the last stitch. This way, the color changes will sit neatly at the bottom center of the body. Round 7 is a bit special. We change to blue yarn in the middle of an increase stitch* ❶ ❷ ❸ ❹. *The last inc of round 7 is worked in 2 colors, with 1 sc in yellow yarn and 1 sc in blue yarn.*
Rnd 7: (sc in next 3 st, inc in next st) repeat 5 times, sc in next 4 st, change to blue yarn, sc in same st as last st [30]
Rnd 8: sc in all 30 st [30]
Rnd 9: sc in next 29 st, change to yellow yarn, sc in next st [30]
Rnd 10: sc in next 29 st, change to blue yarn, sc in next st [30]
Rnd 11: sc in all 30 st [30]
Rnd 12: sc in next 29 st, change to yellow yarn, sc in next st [30]

Insert the safety eyes between rounds 5 and 6, in the stitches you marked earlier.

Rnd 13: sc in all 30 st [30]

Mark the 11th and 16th stitch of round 13 with a stitch marker. In the next round, we'll skip stitches and continue working on a smaller round to make the first part of the body. The skipped stitches will be used to make the second part of the body and the tail later.

Rnd 14: sc in next 5 st, skip next 20 st, sc in next 5 st [10] ⑤

Rnd 15: (sc in next 2 st, dec) repeat 2 times, sc in next 2 st [8]

Rnd 16: sc in next st, dec, sc in next 2 st, dec, sc in next st [6]

Rnd 17: (sc in next st, dec) repeat 2 times [4]

Fasten off, leaving a yarn tail. Using your yarn needle, weave the yarn tail through the front loop of each remaining stitch and pull it tight to close ⑥. Weave in the yarn end.

Continue making the second part of the body. Pull up a loop of yellow yarn in the 16th stitch of round 13 of the body and make a slst ⑦ ⑧ ⑨. Work the first stitch of the next round in the same stitch where you made the slst.

Rnd 14: sc in next 5 st, continue in the 11th stitch of round 14 ⑩, sc in next 5 st [10]

Continue working on this smaller round to make the second part of the body.

Rnd 15: (sc in next 2 st, dec) repeat 2 times, sc in next 2 st [8]

Rnd 16: sc in next st, dec, sc in next 2 st, dec, sc in next st [6]
Rnd 17: (sc in next st, dec) repeat 2 times [4]
Fasten off, leaving a yarn tail. Using your yarn needle, weave the yarn tail through the front loop of each remaining stitch and pull it tight to close. Weave in the yarn tail. Stuff the head and body with fiberfill.

Continue making the tail. Start counting from the first part of the body. Leave a long starting yarn tail and pull up a loop of yellow yarn in the 2nd stitch. Make a slst ⑩. Work the first stitch of the next round in the same stitch where you made the slst.
Rnd 14: sc in next 3 st, count on the other side of the opening, continue in the 2nd stitch, sc in next 3 st [6]
Rnd 15: sc in all 6 st [6]
Rnd 16: inc in all 6 st [12]
Rnd 17: sc in all 12 st [12]
Rnd 18: sc in next st [1] Leave the remaining stitches unworked.
Slst in next st. Fasten off, leaving a long tail for sewing. The tail doesn't need to be stuffed. Vertically fold the tail to flatten it and sew round 18 closed. Weave in the yarn end. If there are small gaps along the sides of the tail, use the starting yarn tail to sew them closed.

FIN *(make 2, in yellow yarn)*

Rnd 1: start 4 sc in a magic ring [4]
Rnd 2: (sc in next st, inc in next st) repeat 2 times [6]
Slst in next st. Fasten off, leaving a long tail for sewing. Flatten the fins and sew round 1 of the fins on the sides of the body, on round 8.

Materials
Sport weight yarn in
- Pink (8 grams)
- Dark pink (leftover)
- Yellow (4 grams)
- Black (leftover)

B-1 / 2.5 mm crochet hook
Yarn needle
Pins
Scissors
Stitch markers
Fiberfill for stuffing

Size
4" / 10 cm tall when made with the indicated yarn

Skills needed
magic ring *(page 17)*
changing color *(page 20)*
fastening off invisible join *(page 19)*

DO YOU WANT TO MAKE A CHENILLE BUTTERFLY?

Materials:
Chenille super bulky weight yarn in
- Pink (24 grams)
- Dark pink (9 grams)
- Yellow (12 grams)
- Black (leftover)

H-8 / 5 mm crochet hook

Size:
This will result in a 8.6" / 22 cm tall butterfly

Scan or visit **www.amigurumi.com/5409** to share pictures and find inspiration in our gallery.

BELLE THE BUTTERFLY

Meet Belle, the happiest little butterfly in your garden. Whenever the sun is out, she flutters through the air, her wings flashing all its bright colors to admiring onlookers. She loves flowery nectar, but she won't say no to a delicious apple slice either. Through their shared love of apples, she has become close friends with Carlo the Caterpillar, and they often share gossip and good food together.

HEAD AND BODY *(start in pink yarn)*

Rnd 1: start 6 sc in a magic ring [6]
Rnd 2: inc in all 6 st [12]
Rnd 3: (sc in next st, inc in next st) repeat 6 times [18]
Rnd 4: (sc in next 2 st, inc in next st) repeat 6 times [24]
Rnd 5: (sc in next 3 st, inc in next st) repeat 6 times [30]
Rnd 6 – 7: sc in all 30 st [30]
Rnd 8: (sc in next 4 st, inc in next st) repeat 6 times [36]
Rnd 9 – 11: sc in all 36 st [36]
Rnd 12: (sc in next 4 st, dec) repeat 6 times [30]
Rnd 13: (sc in next 3 st, dec) repeat 6 times [24]
Rnd 14: (sc in next 2 st, dec) repeat 6 times [18]
Rnd 15: (sc in next 4 st, dec) repeat 3 times [15]

With black yarn, embroider the eyes over rounds 10 and 11, with an interspace of 6 stitches 1 2.
Change to dark pink yarn.
Rnd 16: sc in all 15 st [15]
Rnd 17: (sc in next 2 st, inc in next st) repeat 5 times [20]
Stuff the head and body with fiberfill and continue stuffing as you go. Change to pink yarn.
Rnd 18 – 21: sc in all 20 st [20]
Rnd 22: (sc in next 2 st, dec) repeat 5 times [15]
Rnd 23: (sc in next st, dec) repeat 5 times [10]
Rnd 24: dec 5 times [5]
Fasten off, leaving a yarn tail. Using your yarn needle, weave the yarn tail through the front loop of each remaining stitch and pull it tight to close. Weave in the yarn end.

ANTENNA *(make 2, start in pink yarn)*

Rnd 1: start 6 sc in a magic ring [6]
Rnd 2: (sc in next st, inc in next st) repeat 3 times [9]
Rnd 3: sc in all 9 st [9]
Rnd 4: (sc in next st, dec) repeat 3 times [6]
Change to dark pink yarn.
Rnd 5 – 6: sc in all 6 st [6]
Slst in next st. Fasten off, leaving a long tail for sewing. You can stuff the antenna lightly, but

3

4

5

6

stuffing is optional. Sew the antennae on rounds 4 and 5 of the head, with an interspace of 6 stitches.

WING

Each wing is made with a top and bottom part, which are later sewn together.

Top part of the wing

(make 2, in yellow yarn)

Rnd 1: start 6 sc in a magic ring [6]
Rnd 2: inc in all 6 st [12]
Rnd 3: (sc in next 3 st, inc in next st) repeat 3 times [15]
Rnd 4 – 5: sc in all 15 st [15]
Rnd 6: (sc in next 3 st, dec) repeat 3 times [12]

Rnd 7: sc in all 12 st [12]
Rnd 8: (sc in next 2 st, dec) repeat 3 times [9]
Rnd 9: sc in all 9 st [9]
Rnd 10: (sc in next st, dec) repeat 3 times [6]
Slst in next st. Fasten off, leaving a long tail for sewing. The top parts don't need to be stuffed. Flatten the top parts. Hold both top parts with the last rounds touching each other, and sew them together 3 4.

Bottom part of the wing

(make 2, in yellow yarn)

Rnd 1: start 6 sc in a magic ring [6]
Rnd 2: inc in all 6 st [12]
Rnd 3 – 4: sc in all 12 st [12]
Rnd 5: (sc in next 2 st, dec) repeat 3 times [9]
Rnd 6: sc in all 9 st [9]
Rnd 7: (sc in next st, dec) repeat 3 times [6]
Slst in next st. The bottom parts don't need to be stuffed. Fasten off, leaving a yarn tail. Using your yarn needle, weave the yarn tail through the front loop of each remaining stitch and pull it tight to close. Sew the bottom wing parts to rounds 7-10 of the top wing parts, at an angle 5 6.

WING DOT *(make 4, in dark pink yarn)*

Rnd 1: start 6 sc in a magic ring [6]
Fasten off with an invisible join, leaving a long tail for sewing. Sew the dots on the top part of the wings (on both the back and the front side), over rounds 3 and 4. Sew the middle of the wings to the back of the body, over rounds 16-20.

Materials
Sport weight yarn in
Gray (10 grams)
B-1 / 2.5 mm crochet hook
Safety eyes (6 mm)
Yarn needle
Pins
Scissors
Stitch markers
Fiberfill for stuffing

Size
4.7" / 12 cm long when made with the indicated yarn

Skills needed
magic ring *(page 17)*
crocheting in rows *(page 11)*

DO YOU WANT TO MAKE A CHENILLE HIPPO?

Materials:
Chenille super bulky weight yarn in
Gray (30 grams)
H-8 / 5 mm crochet hook
Safety eyes (15 mm)

Size:
This will result in a 9.4" / 24 cm long hippo

Scan or visit **www.amigurumi.com/5410** to share pictures and find inspiration in our gallery.

NORA THE HIPPO

Nora the Hippo loves crocheting. She makes long scarves for her giraffe friends and cosy hats for her monkey pals. One day, she started crocheting a blanket, got lost in her thoughts and ended up making the biggest blanket anyone had ever seen. Now Nora takes it out on summer nights, when her friends stay up late to watch the stars, so everyone can snuggle together.

HEAD AND BODY *(in gray yarn)*

Rnd 1: start 6 sc in a magic ring [6]
Rnd 2: inc in all 6 st [12]
Rnd 3: (sc in next st, inc in next st) repeat 6 times [18]
Rnd 4: (sc in next 2 st, inc in next st) repeat 6 times [24]
Rnd 5: (sc in next 7 st, inc in next st) repeat 3 times [27]
Rnd 6 – 13: sc in all 27 st [27]
Insert the safety eyes between rounds 2 and 3, with an interspace of 4 stitches.
Rnd 14: (sc in next 7 st, dec) repeat 3 times [24]
Stuff the head and body with fiberfill and continue stuffing as you go.
Rnd 15: (sc in next 2 st, dec) repeat 6 times [18]
Rnd 16: (sc in next st, dec) repeat 6 times [12]
Rnd 17: dec 6 times [6]
Fasten off, leaving a yarn tail. Using your yarn needle, weave the yarn tail through the front loop of each remaining stitch and pull it tight to close. Weave in the yarn end.

SNOUT *(in gray yarn)*

Rnd 1: start 6 sc in a magic ring [6]
Rnd 2: inc in all 6 st [12]
Rnd 3: (sc in next st, inc in next st) repeat 6 times [18]
Rnd 4 – 5: sc in all 18 st [18]
Rnd 6: (sc in next 3 st, dec, sc in next 2 st, dec) repeat 2 times [14]
Fasten off, leaving a long tail for sewing. With gray yarn, embroider the nostrils between rounds

4 and 5 of the snout. Each nostril is 1 stitch wide 1 2. Sew the snout to the head with the nostrils at the top. Sew it over the magic ring, with the top just below round 2 (touching the safety eyes) and the bottom above round 6. Stuff the snout lightly with fiberfill before closing the seam.

EAR *(make 2, in gray yarn)*

Rnd 1: start 3 sc in a magic ring, ch 1, turn [3] 3
Continue crocheting in rows.
Row 2: inc in all 3 st [6]
Fasten off, leaving a long tail for sewing 4. Pinch the ear together and sew it together with a few stitches 5 6. Sew the ears 3 rounds above the eyes, with an interspace of 5 stitches.

LEG *(make 4, in gray yarn)*

Rnd 1: start 6 sc in a magic ring [6]
Rnd 2: sc in all 6 st [6]
Fasten off, leaving a long tail for sewing.
Sew the legs to the bottom of the body. Sew the front legs over rounds 8-9, with an interspace of 4 stitches. Sew the hind legs over rounds 13-14, with an interspace of 3 stitches.

TAIL *(in gray yarn)*

Ch 4. Crochet in rows.
Row 1: start in second ch from hook, slst in next 3 ch [3]
Fasten off, leaving a long tail for sewing. Sew the tail to the back of the body, between rounds 15 and 16.

Materials
Sport weight yarn in
- Yellow (8 grams)
- Black (leftover)
- White (4 grams)

B-1 / 2.5 mm crochet hook
Safety eyes (8 mm)
Yarn needle
Pins
Scissors
Stitch markers
Fiberfill for stuffing

Size
4" / 10 cm tall when made with the indicated yarn

Skills needed
magic ring *(page 17)*
changing color *(page 20)*

DO YOU WANT TO MAKE A CHENILLE BEE?

Materials:
Chenille super bulky weight yarn in
- Yellow (24 grams)
- Black (9 grams)
- White (12 grams)

H-8 / 5 mm crochet hook
Safety eyes (18 mm)

Size:
This will result in a 8.3" / 21 cm tall bee

Scan or visit **www.amigurumi.com/5411** to share pictures and find inspiration in our gallery.

BUZZY THE BEE

Buzzy the Bee loves humans, or to be more precise, he loves humans carrying picnic baskets. He'll wait until all the delicious food has been put down on the blanket before buzzing by and trying to get a taste. Sandwiches and lemonade are always a winner, but his absolute favorite is strawberry cheesecake. It's too bad some humans confuse him with a wasp and get all panicky, little Buzzy really means no harm and just wants to join in the fun.

HEAD AND BODY *(start in yellow yarn)*

Rnd 1: start 6 sc in a magic ring [6]
Rnd 2: inc in all 6 st [12]
Rnd 3: (sc in next st, inc in next st) repeat 6 times [18]
Rnd 4: (sc in next 2 st, inc in next st) repeat 6 times [24]
Rnd 5: (sc in next 3 st, inc in next st) repeat 6 times [30]
Rnd 6 – 7: sc in all 30 st [30]
Rnd 8: (sc in next 4 st, inc in next st) repeat 6 times [36]
Rnd 9 – 11: sc in all 36 st [36]
Rnd 12: (sc in next 4 st, dec) repeat 6 times [30]
Rnd 13: (sc in next 3 st, dec) repeat 6 times [24]
Rnd 14: (sc in next 2 st, dec) repeat 6 times [18]
Continue crocheting in a stripe pattern, alternating 1 round in black yarn and 1 round in yellow yarn. The color change is indicated before each round.
Rnd 15: (black) sc in all 18 st [18]
Insert the safety eyes between rounds 8 and 9, with an interspace of 5 stitches.
Rnd 16: (yellow) (sc in next 2 st, inc in next st) repeat 6 times [24]
Rnd 17: (black) sc in all 24 st [24]
Rnd 18: (yellow) sc in all 24 st [24]
Rnd 19: (black) sc in all 24 st [24]
Rnd 20: (yellow) sc in all 24 st [24]
Rnd 21: (black) (sc in next 2 st, dec) repeat 6 times [18]
Continue crocheting in black yarn. Stuff the head and body with fiberfill and continue stuffing as you go.
Rnd 22: (sc in next st, dec) repeat 6 times [12]
Rnd 23: dec 6 times [6]
Rnd 24: (sc in next st, dec) repeat 2 times [4]
Fasten off, leaving a yarn tail. Using your yarn needle, weave the yarn tail through the front loop of each remaining stitch and pull it tight to close. Weave in the yarn end.

WING *(make 2, in white yarn)*

Rnd 1: start 6 sc in a magic ring [6]
Rnd 2: inc in all 6 st [12]
Rnd 3: (sc in next 3 st, inc in next st) repeat 3 times [15]
Rnd 4 – 5: sc in all 15 st [15]
Rnd 6: (sc in next 3 st, dec) repeat 3 times [12]

Rnd 7: (sc in next 2 st, dec) repeat 3 times [9]
Rnd 8: (sc in next st, dec) repeat 3 times [6]
Slst in next st. Fasten off, leaving a long tail for sewing. The wings don't need to be stuffed. Flatten the wings. Hold both wings with the last rounds touching each other, and sew them together ❶ ❷. Pinch the middle of the wings and sew it together with a few stitches ❸. Sew the middle of the wings to the back of the body, over rounds 16-17 ❹.

ANTENNA *(make 2, start in yellow yarn)*

Rnd 1: start 6 sc in a magic ring [6]
Rnd 2: (sc in next st, inc in next st) repeat 3 times [9]
Rnd 3: sc in all 9 st [9]
Rnd 4: (sc in next st, dec) repeat 3 times [6]
Change to black yarn.
Rnd 5 – 6: sc in all 6 st [6]
Slst in next st. Fasten off, leaving a long tail for sewing. You can stuff the antenna lightly, but stuffing is optional. Sew the antennae on round 3 of the head, with an interspace of 4 stitches.

Materials
Sport weight yarn in
- Gray (4 grams)
- Light gray (7 grams)
- Dark gray (leftover)
- White (leftover)
- Black (leftover)

B-1 / 2.5 mm crochet hook
Safety eyes (7 mm)
Yarn needle
Pins
Scissors
Stitch markers
Fiberfill for stuffing

Size
2.4" / 6 cm tall when made with the indicated yarn

Skills needed
magic ring *(page 17)*
changing color *(page 20)*

DO YOU WANT TO MAKE A CHENILLE PIGEON?

Materials:
Chenille super bulky weight yarn in
- Gray (12 grams)
- Light gray (21 grams)
- Dark gray (6 grams)
- White (6 grams)
- Black (6 grams)

H-8 / 5 mm crochet hook
Safety eyes (15 mm)

Size:
This will result in a 4.7" / 12 cm tall pigeon

Scan or visit **www.amigurumi.com/5412** to share pictures and find inspiration in our gallery.

DEXTER THE PIGEON

Dexter the pigeon recently moved to Amsterdam and while he loves to watch the boats on the canals, he clearly underestimated just how much walking he'd need to do to get from one place to another. You see, Dexter doesn't like heights, which puts him at quite a disadvantage when it comes to flying. His friend Oliver the Mouse happily drew him a map of all the relevant bridges and the best spots to find crumbs, so now he can navigate the city's waterways with ease.

HEAD AND BODY *(start in gray yarn)*

Rnd 1: start 6 sc in a magic ring [6]
Rnd 2: inc in all 6 st [12]
Rnd 3: (sc in next st, inc in next st) repeat 6 times [18]
Rnd 4: (sc in next 5 st, inc in next st) repeat 3 times [21]

Mark the 7th and 14th stitch of round 4 with a stitch marker.

Rnd 5 – 8: sc in all 21 st [21]

Change to dark gray yarn (1) (2) (3).

Rnd 9: (sc in next 6 st, inc in next st) repeat 3 times [24]

Insert the safety eyes between rounds 4 and 5, in the stitches you marked earlier. Change to light gray yarn. In the next round, we'll make chains to create the 'spine' of the pigeon's back.

Rnd 10: slst in next st (4) (5), ch 4 (6), start in second ch from hook, sc in next 3 ch (7), sc in same st on the body where you made the slst, continue on the body, sc in next 4 st (8), inc in next st, sc in next 12 st, inc in next st, sc in next 5 st [30]
Rnd 11: sc in the other side of next 3 ch, inc in next st, sc in next 28 st [33]
Rnd 12 – 14: sc in all 33 st [33]
Rnd 15: sc in next 9 st, (dec, sc in next 2 st) repeat 6 times [27]
Rnd 16: sc in next st, dec 3 times, sc in next 2 st, (dec, sc in next st) repeat 6 times [18]

Stuff the head and body firmly with fiberfill and continue stuffing as you go.

Rnd 17: (sc in next st, dec) repeat 6 times [12]
Rnd 18: dec 6 times [6]

Fasten off, leaving a yarn tail. Using your yarn needle, weave the yarn tail through the front loop of each remaining stitch and pull it tight to close. Weave in the yarn end.

WING *(make 2, start in light gray yarn)*

Rnd 1: start 6 sc in a magic ring [6]
Rnd 2: (sc in next st, inc in next st) repeat 3 times [9]
Rnd 3: sc in all 9 st [9]
Change to dark gray yarn.
Rnd 4: sc in all 9 st [9]
Change to light gray yarn.
Rnd 5: (sc in next st, dec) repeat 3 times [6]
Change to dark gray yarn.
Rnd 6: (sc in next st, dec) repeat 2 times [4]
Fasten off, leaving a yarn tail. The wings don't need to be stuffed. Using your yarn needle, weave the yarn tail through the front loop of each remaining stitch and pull it tight to close. Leave a long tail for sewing. Sew the wings on the sides of the body, between rounds 11-13. The tip of the wings is pointing towards the back of the body. Sew all around the wings, but leave the tip unsewn.

BEAK *(start in black yarn)*

Rnd 1: start 5 sc in a magic ring [5]
Change to white yarn.
Rnd 2: sc in all 5 st [5]
Slst in next st. Fasten off, leaving a long tail for sewing. Sew the beak over rounds 5 and 6 of the head, centered between the eyes.

Materials
Sport weight yarn in
  Beige (leftover)
  Light brown (11 grams)
  Dark brown (leftover)
  Black (leftover)
B-1 / 2.5 mm crochet hook
Safety eyes (7 mm)
Yarn needle
Pins
Scissors
Stitch markers
Fiberfill for stuffing

Size
3.5" / 9 cm long when made with the indicated yarn

Skills needed
magic ring *(page 17)*
changing color *(page 20)*
crocheting around a foundation chain *(page 18)*
fastening off invisible join *(page 19)*

DO YOU WANT TO MAKE A CHENILLE SLOTH?

Materials:
Chenille super bulky weight yarn in
  Beige (6 grams)
  Light brown (33 grams)
  Dark brown (6 grams)
  Black (leftover)
H-8 / 5 mm crochet hook
Safety eyes (14 mm)

Size:
This will result in a 8.6" / 22 cm long sloth

Scan or visit **www.amigurumi.com/5413** to share pictures and find inspiration in our gallery.

ARLO THE SLOTH

Arlo the Sloth has a knack for origami. Though his movements are slow, his long fingers fold paper with delicate precision. Each day, he creates animal origami – cranes, frogs, and tigers – and uses them to adorn his favorite branch. Jungle visitors like to walk over to his tree, marveling at his hanging art gallery. Arlo knows that slow is smooth, and smooth is fast.

1

2

3

4

EYE SPOT *(make 2, in dark brown yarn)*

Ch 5. Stitches are worked around both sides of the foundation chain.

Rnd 1: start in second ch from hook, sc in next 3 st, 4 sc in next st. Continue on the other side of the foundation chain, sc in next 2 st, 3 sc in last st [12]

Fasten off with an invisible join, leaving a long tail for sewing. Insert the safety eye through a stitch on the side of the eye spot, but don't close the washer yet 1.

HEAD AND BODY *(start in beige yarn)*

Rnd 1: start 6 sc in a magic ring [6]

Rnd 2: inc in all 6 st [12]

Rnd 3: (sc in next st, inc in next st) repeat 6 times [18]

Mark the 2nd and 7th stitch of round 3 with a stitch marker.

Rnd 4: (sc in next 2 st, inc in next st) repeat 6 times [24]

Rnd 5: sc in all 24 st [24]

Change to light brown yarn.

Rnd 6: (sc in next 3 st, inc in next st) repeat 6 times [30]

Rnd 7 – 10: sc in all 30 st [30]

Position the eye spots on the head, between rounds 3 and 4, and insert the safety eyes in the stitches you marked earlier 2 3. Position the eye spots on the head. Close the washers, but don't sew the eye spots to the head yet.

With black yarn, embroider the nose over round 1 of the head, the nose is 2 stitches wide 4 5.

Rnd 11: (sc in next 3 st, dec) repeat 6 times [24]

Rnd 12: (sc in next st, dec) repeat 8 times [16]

Rnd 13: sc in all 16 st [16]
Rnd 14: (sc in next 3 st, inc in next st) repeat 4 times [20]
Rnd 15: sc in all 20 st [20]
Stuff the head and body with fiberfill and continue stuffing as you go.
Rnd 16: (sc in next 4 st, inc in next st) repeat 4 times [24]
Rnd 17 – 19: sc in all 24 st [24]
Rnd 20: (sc in next 2 st, dec) repeat 6 times [18]
Rnd 21: (sc in next st, dec) repeat 6 times [12]
Rnd 22: dec 6 times [6]
Fasten off, leaving a yarn tail. Using your yarn needle, weave the yarn tail through the front loop of each remaining stitch and pull it tight to close. Weave in the yarn end. Sew the eye spots to the head.

LEG *(make 4, in light brown yarn)*

Rnd 1: start 6 sc in a magic ring [6]
Rnd 2: (sc in next 2 st, inc in next st) repeat 2 times [8]
Rnd 3 – 5: sc in all 8 st [8]
Rnd 6: (sc in next 2 st, dec) repeat 2 times [6]
Rnd 7 – 8: sc in all 6 st [6]
Slst in next st. Fasten off, leaving a long tail for sewing. Stuff the legs lightly with fiberfill. With beige yarn, embroider 3 nails on round 2 of each leg 6 7. Each nail is 1 round long. Sew 2 front legs over rounds 14-15, with an interspace of 5 stitches across the belly. Sew 2 hind legs over rounds 20-21, with an interspace of 4 stitches across the belly 8.

Materials
Sport weight yarn in
  Blue (8 grams)
  Green (leftover)
  Black (leftover)
B-1 / 2.5 mm crochet hook
Yarn needle
Pins
Scissors
Stitch markers
Fiberfill for stuffing

Size
2.5" / 6.5 cm long when made with the indicated yarn

Skills needed
magic ring *(page 17)*
half double crochet *(page 15)*
double crochet *(page 15)*

DO YOU WANT TO MAKE A CHENILLE WHALE?

Materials:
Chenille super bulky weight yarn in
  Blue (24 grams)
  Green (9 grams)
  Black (leftover)
H-8 / 5 mm crochet hook

Size:
This will result in a 6" / 15 cm long whale

Scan or visit **www.amigurumi.com/5414** to share pictures and find inspiration in our gallery.

BLUB THE WHALE

Blub the Whale sometimes feels a bit blue, without really knowing why. His fish friends try to cheer him up, and there's one thing that always works: they'll search for a boat filled with whale watchers, and persuade Blub to take one big leap out of the water. The onlookers always gasp in wonder and delight, shouting 'Perfect!', 'Magnificent!' and 'Have you ever seen such beauty?'. And with these words of praise lighting up his heart, Blub will happily swim along.

HEAD AND BODY *(in blue yarn)*

Rnd 1: start 6 sc in a magic ring [6]
Rnd 2: inc in all 6 st [12]
Rnd 3: (sc in next st, inc in next st) repeat 6 times [18]
Rnd 4: (sc in next 2 st, inc in next st) repeat 6 times [24]
Rnd 5 – 7: sc in all 24 st [24]
Mark the 4th and 19th stitch of round 7 with a stitch marker.
Rnd 8 – 10: sc in all 24 st [24]
With black yarn, embroider the eyes between rounds 7 and 8, using the marked stitches as a guide 1.
Rnd 11: sc in next 6 st, dec 6 times, sc in next 6 st [18]
Rnd 12: sc in next 5 st, dec 2 times, sc in next st, dec 2 times, sc in next 4 st [14]
Rnd 13: sc in next 5 st, dec, sc in next st, dec, sc in next 4 st [12]
Rnd 14: sc in next 4 st, dec 3 times, sc in next 2 st [9]
Stuff the head and body with fiberfill and continue stuffing as you go.
Rnd 15: sc in all 9 st [9]
Rnd 16: dec, sc in next 7 st [8]
Fasten off and weave in the yarn end.

FIN *(make 2, in blue yarn)*

Rnd 1: start 4 sc in a magic ring [4]
Rnd 2: sc in next st, inc in next st, sc in next 2 st [5]
Rnd 3: sc in all 5 st [5]
Slst in next st. Fasten off, leaving a long tail for sewing. The fins don't need to be stuffed. Sew the fins on the sides of the body, between rounds 9 and 12.

TAIL FIN *(make 2, in blue yarn)*

Rnd 1: start 4 sc in a magic ring [4]
Rnd 2: (sc in next st, inc in next st) repeat 2 times [6]
Rnd 3: sc in all 6 st [6]

4

5

6

Rnd 4: (sc in next st, dec) repeat 2 times [4]
Slst in next st. Fasten off, leaving a long tail for sewing. The tail fins don't need to be stuffed. Sew the tail fins horizontally on the last round of the body, right next to each other 2 3.

BELLY *(in green yarn)*

Rnd 1: start 6 sc in a magic ring [6]
Rnd 2: inc in all 6 st [12]
Rnd 3: (sc in next st, inc in next st) repeat 6 times [18]
Rnd 4: sc in next st, hdc in next st, hdc + dc + hdc in next st, hdc in next st, sc in next st [7]
Leave the remaining stitches unworked.
Slst in next st. Fasten off, leaving a long tail for sewing. Sew the belly on the bottom side of the whale's body, with the top just below round 3 and the bottom above round 13 4 5 6. The tip of the belly is pointing towards the tail.

Materials
Sport weight yarn in
  Orange (10 grams)
  White (leftover)
B-1 / 2.5 mm crochet hook
Safety eyes (one 6 mm and one 8 mm eye, since the octopus has a big and small eye)
Yarn needle
Pins
Scissors
Stitch markers
Fiberfill for stuffing

Size
2" / 5 cm tall when made with the indicated yarn

Skills needed
magic ring *(page 17)*
fastening off invisible join *(page 19)*

DO YOU WANT TO MAKE A CHENILLE OCTOPUS?

Materials:
Chenille super bulky weight yarn in
  Orange (30 grams)
  White (6 grams)
H-8 / 5 mm crochet hook
Safety eyes (one 14 mm and one 18 mm, since the octopus has a big and small eye)

Size:
This will result in a 4.7" / 12 cm tall octopus

Scan or visit **www.amigurumi.com/5415** to share pictures and find inspiration in our gallery.

BUBBLES THE OCTOPUS

Bubbles' parents named him after his favorite thing in the whole world: bubble baths! When he was just a baby octopus, he loved bath time so much that his parents would bring him snacks while he happily splashed away in the tub. On his first birthday, a kind dolphin gifted him a discarded bubble wand and now Bubbles can create bubbly magic wherever he goes.

BIG EYE *(in white yarn)*

Rnd 1: start 10 sc in a magic ring [10]
Fasten off with an invisible join, leaving a long tail for sewing. Insert the bigger safety eye through the magic ring, but don't close the washer yet.

SMALL EYE *(in white yarn)*

Rnd 1: start 6 sc in a magic ring [6]
Fasten off with an invisible join, leaving a long tail for sewing. Insert the smaller safety eye through the magic ring, but don't close the washer yet.

TENTACLE *(make 8, in orange yarn)*

Rnd 1: start 6 sc in a magic ring [6]
Rnd 2: (sc in next st, inc in next st) repeat 3 times [9]
Rnd 3: (sc in next st, dec) repeat 3 times [6]
Slst in next st. Fasten off and weave in the yarn end. The tentacles don't need to be stuffed.

HEAD AND BODY *(in orange yarn)*

Rnd 1: start 8 sc in a magic ring [8]
Rnd 2: inc in all 8 st [16]
Rnd 3: (sc in next st, inc in next st) repeat 8 times [24]
Rnd 4: (sc in next 3 st, inc in next st) repeat 6 times [30]
Rnd 5: sc in all 30 st [30]
Rnd 6: (sc in next 4 st, inc in next st) repeat 6 times [36]
Rnd 7 – 11: sc in all 36 st [36]
Rnd 12: (sc in next 4 st, dec) repeat 6 times [30]
Rnd 13: sc in all 30 st [30]
Rnd 14: (sc in next 3 st, dec) repeat 6 times [24]
Insert the safety eyes with the white eyes between rounds 11 and 12, with an interspace

of 2 stitches. The white eyes touch in the middle. Close the washers, but don't sew the white eyes to the head yet.

Note: *In the next round, we'll join the tentacles to the body. Flatten each tentacle and hold it next to the body. To attach them, you work the next stitches through both layers of the tentacle and the body (so working through 3 layers at once).*

Rnd 15: (work through both a flattened tentacle and the body: sc in next 3 st) repeat 8 times [24] 1 2 3

Rnd 16: (sc in next st, dec) repeat 8 times [16]

Stuff the head and body with fiberfill.

Rnd 17: dec 8 times [8]

Fasten off, leaving a yarn tail. Using your yarn needle, weave the yarn tail through the front loop of each remaining stitch and pull it tight to close. Weave in the yarn end. Sew the white eyes to the head.

Materials
Sport weight yarn in
Green (12 grams)
Yellow (4 grams)
Red (leftover)
B-1 / 2.5 mm crochet hook
Safety eyes (6 mm)
Yarn needle
Pins
Scissors
Stitch markers
Fiberfill for stuffing
Optional: metal wire/pipe cleaner

Size
8.3" / 21 cm long when made with the indicated yarn

Skills needed
magic ring *(page 17)*
crocheting in rows *(page 11)*
fastening off invisible join *(page 19)*

DO YOU WANT TO MAKE A CHENILLE SNAKE?

Materials:
Chenille super bulky weight yarn in
Green (36 grams)
Yellow (12 grams)
Red (leftover)
H-8 / 5 mm crochet hook
Safety eyes (14 mm)

Size:
This will result in a 19.6" / 50 cm long snake.

Scan or visit **www.amigurumi.com/5416** to share pictures and find inspiration in our gallery.

ALEX THE SNAKE

Alex the Snake has a love – for bread. While most snakes hunt for mice, Alex slithers to the local bakery, patiently queuing and waiting until it's his turn to order. He loves whole wheat and sourdough bread, but he won't say no to a brioche or a focaccia. And when the day is really getting him down, he'll get a chocolate croissant as well, because there's nothing that buttery flakiness can't solve!

TONGUE *(in red yarn)*

Ch 3. Crochet in rows.

Row 1: start in second ch from hook, sc in next 2 ch [2]

Fasten off, leaving a long tail for sewing.

HEAD AND BODY *(in green yarn)*

Rnd 1: start 6 sc in a magic ring [6]

Rnd 2: inc in all 6 st [12]

Rnd 3: sc in all 12 st [12]

Rnd 4: (sc in next st, inc in next st) repeat 6 times [18]

Mark the 5th and 13th stitch of round 4 with a stitch marker.

Rnd 5: sc in all 18 st [18]

Rnd 6: (sc in next 2 st, inc in next st) repeat 6 times [24]

Rnd 7 – 8: sc in all 24 st [24]

Insert the safety eyes between rounds 4 and 5, in the stitches you marked earlier. Sew the tongue on round 3 of the head ❶ and knot it on the inside ❷.

Rnd 9: (sc in next 3 st, dec 3 times, sc in next 3 st) repeat 2 times [18]

Rnd 10: (sc in next 2 st, dec 2 times, sc in next 3 st) repeat 2 times [14]

Rnd 11: (sc in next st, dec 2 times, sc in next 2 st) repeat 2 times [10]

Rnd 12: sc in all 10 st [10]

3

4

5

Take the metal wire or pipe cleaner and bend one end to look like a lasso 3. Insert the bended end into the snake's head 4. Stuff the head with fiberfill and continue stuffing the head and body as you go. Continue crocheting around the metal wire or pipe cleaner 5.

Rnd 13: sc in next 8 st, dec [9]
Rnd 14 – 51: sc in all 9 st [9]
Rnd 52: sc in next 7 st, dec [8]
Rnd 53 – 54: sc in all 8 st [8]
Rnd 55: (sc in next 2 st, dec) repeat 2 times [6]

Bend the other end of the metal wire or pipe cleaner into a tiny loop to avoid sharp edges.
Fasten off, leaving a yarn tail. Using your yarn needle, weave the yarn tail through the front loop of each remaining stitch and pull it tight to close. Weave in the yarn end.

BIG SPOT *(make 3, in yellow yarn)*

Rnd 1: start 6 sc in a magic ring [6]
Fasten off with an invisible join, leaving a long tail for sewing.

SMALL SPOT
(make 3, in yellow yarn)

Rnd 1: start 4 sc in a magic ring [4]
Fasten off with an invisible join, leaving a long tail for sewing.
Pin and sew the big and small spots on the body. Bend the snake into a fun shape.

Materials
Sport weight yarn in
Beige (4 grams)
Red brown (11 grams)
Black (leftover)
B-1 / 2.5 mm crochet hook
Yarn needle
Pins
Scissors
Stitch markers
Fiberfill for stuffing

Size
2.7" / 7 cm long when made with the indicated yarn

Skills needed
magic ring *(page 17)*

DO YOU WANT TO MAKE A CHENILLE SQUIRREL?

Materials:
Chenille super bulky weight yarn in
Beige (12 grams)
Red brown (33 grams)
Black (leftover)
H-8 / 5 mm crochet hook

Size:
This will result in a 6" / 15 cm long squirrel

Scan or visit **www.amigurumi.com/5417** to share pictures and find inspiration in our gallery.

SASHA THE SQUIRREL

Her squirrel friends don't mind the rustic interior of their nest, but Sasha prefers to decorate every surface of hers with bright, downy feathers. You can see her darting through the forest, picking up discarded feathers or bargaining with particularly beautiful birds to get a feather or two. Maybe Cara the Cockatiel will gift her a feather as well, in return for some tasty nuts?

HEAD AND BODY *(in red brown yarn)*

Rnd 1: start 6 sc in a magic ring [6]
Rnd 2: inc in all 6 st [12]
Rnd 3: (sc in next st, inc in next st) repeat 6 times [18]
Mark the 5th and 14th stitch of round 3 with a stitch marker.
Rnd 4: (sc in next 2 st, inc in next st) repeat 6 times [24]
Rnd 5: (sc in next 7 st, inc in next st) repeat 3 times [27]
Rnd 6 – 13: sc in all 27 st [27]
With black yarn, embroider the eyes over rounds 3-4, using the marked stitches as a guide.
Rnd 14: (sc in next 7 st, dec) repeat 3 times [24]
Rnd 15: (sc in next 2 st, dec) repeat 6 times [18]
Stuff the head and body with fiberfill and continue stuffing as you go.
Rnd 16: (sc in next st, dec) repeat 6 times [12]
Rnd 17: dec 6 times [6]
Fasten off, leaving a yarn tail. Using your yarn needle, weave the yarn tail through the front loop of each remaining stitch and pull it tight to close. Weave in the yarn end.

SNOUT *(in beige yarn)*

Rnd 1: start 6 sc in a magic ring [6]
Rnd 2: (sc in next st, inc in next st) repeat 3 times [9]
Rnd 3: sc in all 9 st [9]
Fasten off, leaving a long tail for sewing. With black yarn, embroider the nose between rounds 1 and 2 of

5

6

7

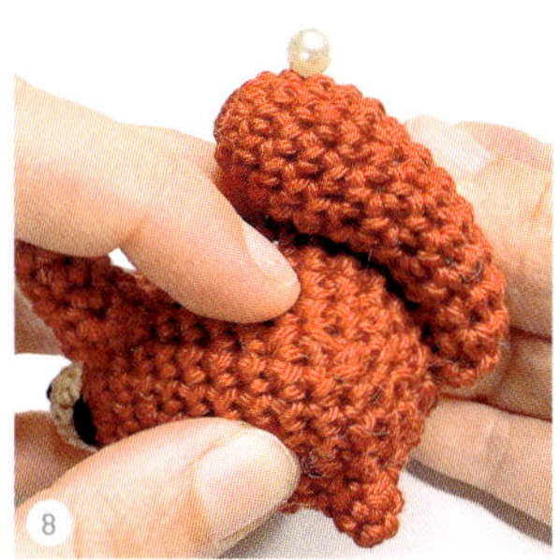
8

the snout. The nose is 1 stitch wide.
Sew the snout onto the head, centered over the magic ring, with the top positioned just below round 2 and the bottom just above round 4, right between the eyes 1 2. Stuff the snout lightly with fiberfill before closing the seam.

EAR *(make 2, in red brown yarn)*

Rnd 1: start 4 sc in a magic ring [4]
Rnd 2: (sc in next st, inc in next st) repeat 2 times [6]
Rnd 3: sc in all 6 st [6]
Rnd 4: (sc in next 2 st, inc in next st) repeat 2 times [8]
Rnd 5: sc in all 8 st [8]
Slst in next st. Fasten off, leaving a long tail for sewing. The ears don't need to be stuffed 3. Flatten the ears. With beige yarn, embroider 3 stripes over rounds 2-5 of each ear 4. Pinch and sew the ear together at the bottom with a few stitches to keep its shape 5 6. Sew the ears to rounds 6-7 of the head, with an interspace of 6 stitches 7.

LEG *(make 4, in red brown yarn)*

Rnd 1: start 4 sc in a magic ring [4]
Rnd 2: (sc in next st, inc in next st) repeat 2 times [6]
Fasten off, leaving a long tail for sewing. Sew the legs to the bottom of the body. Sew the front legs over rounds 8-9, with an interspace of 4 stitches across the belly. Sew the hind legs over rounds 13-14, with an interspace of 3 stitches across the belly.

TAIL *(in red brown yarn)*

Rnd 1: start 6 sc in a magic ring [6]
Rnd 2: inc in all 6 st [12]
Rnd 3 – 6: sc in all 12 st [12]
Rnd 7: (sc in next 2 st, dec) repeat 3 times [9]
Rnd 8 – 10: sc in all 9 st [9]
Rnd 11: (sc in next st, dec) repeat 3 times [6]
Rnd 12 – 13: sc in all 6 st [6]
Fasten off, leaving a long tail for sewing. Stuff the tail with fiberfill. Sew the tail on the back of the body, over rounds 12-17 8.

Materials
Sport weight yarn in
Gray (13 grams)
White (leftover)
Black (leftover)
B-1 / 2.5 mm crochet hook
Safety eyes (8 mm)
Yarn needle
Pins
Scissors
Stitch markers
Fiberfill for stuffing

Size
4" / 10 cm long when made with the indicated yarn

Skills needed
magic ring *(page 17)*
joining parts – crocheting pieces together *(page 22)*

DO YOU WANT TO MAKE A CHENILLE SEAL?

Materials:
Chenille super bulky weight yarn in
Gray (39 grams)
White (9 grams)
Black (leftover)
H-8 / 5 mm crochet hook
Safety eyes (18 mm)

Size:
This will result in a 10" / 25 cm long seal

Scan or visit **www.amigurumi.com/5418** to share pictures and find inspiration in our gallery.

SULLY THE SEAL

Sully is a playful little seal, and his favorite toy is a bouncy ball. Balancing it on his nose is one of his best tricks, along with launching it high into the air with a quick swipe of his tail. He keeps losing toys, though, as a strong sea current carries them off on new adventures. So for his birthday, all of his friends chipped in and bought him a lightweight buoy to play with.

HEAD AND BODY *(in gray yarn)*

Rnd 1: start 8 sc in a magic ring [8]
Rnd 2: inc in all 8 st [16]
Rnd 3: (sc in next st, inc in next st) repeat 8 times [24]
Mark the 9th and 18th stitch of round 3 with a stitch marker.
Rnd 4: (sc in next 3 st, inc in next st) repeat 6 times [30]
Rnd 5: sc in all 30 st [30]
Rnd 6: (sc in next 4 st, inc in next st) repeat 6 times [36]
Rnd 7 – 10: sc in all 36 st [36]
Insert the safety eyes between rounds 3 and 4, in the stitches you marked earlier.
Rnd 11: sc in next 11 st, dec, sc in next 3 st, dec, sc in next 4 st, dec, sc in next 3 st, dec, sc in next 7 st [32]
Rnd 12: sc in next 14 st, dec, sc in next 4 st, dec, sc in next 10 st [30]
Rnd 13: sc in all 30 st [30]
Stuff the head and body with fiberfill and continue stuffing as you go.
Rnd 14: (sc in next 3 st, dec) repeat 6 times [24]
Rnd 15 – 19: sc in all 24 st [24]
Rnd 20: (sc in next 2 st, dec) repeat 6 times [18]
Rnd 21: sc in all 18 st [18]
Rnd 22: (sc in next st, dec) repeat 6 times [12]
Slst in next st. Fasten off and weave in the yarn end.

TAIL *(in gray yarn)*

Start by making 2 separate tail fins.

Tail fin *(make 2, in gray yarn)*

Rnd 1: start 4 sc in a magic ring [4]
Rnd 2: (sc in next st, inc in next st) repeat 2 times [6]
Rnd 3: (sc in next st, inc in next st) repeat 3 times [9]
Rnd 4 – 5: sc in all 9 st [9]
Rnd 6: (sc in next st, dec) repeat 3 times [6]
Fasten off on the first tail fin and weave in the yarn end. Don't fasten off on the second tail fin. The tail fins don't need to be stuffed. In the next round, we'll join the fins together to make the tail.

Joining the fins

Rnd 7: sc in next 3 st on the second fin, continue in the first stitch of the first fin ❶, sc in next 6 st on the first fin, continue in the fourth stitch of the second fin ❷, sc in next 3 st [12]

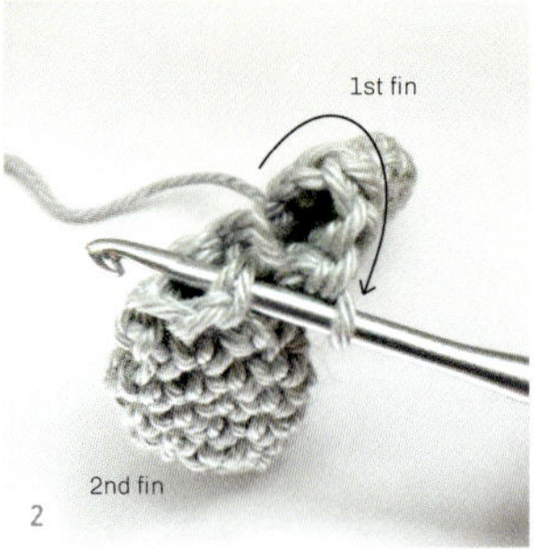

Rnd 8: sc in all 12 st [12]
Slst in next st. Fasten off, leaving a long tail for sewing ❸. Sew round 8 of the tail to round 22 of the body ❹, adding more fiberfill to the body before closing the seam ❺. Make sure the fins are aligned horizontally in relation to the eyes, when sewing the tail to the body.

SNOUT *(make 2 parts, in white yarn)*

Rnd 1: start 6 sc in a magic ring [6]
Rnd 2: sc in all 6 st [6]
Rnd 3: sc in next 2 st, inc in next st, sc in next 3 st [7]
Fasten off and weave in the yarn end on the first part. Don't fasten off on the second part but leave a long tail for sewing.
Position both snout parts with the last rounds touching each other, and sew them together ❻. With black yarn, embroider a small nose in the middle of the snout, the nose is 1 stitch wide ❼. Sew the snout to rounds 1-2 of the head, just below the magic ring center.

FIN *(make 2, in gray yarn)*

Rnd 1: start 6 sc in a magic ring [6]
Rnd 2: (sc in next st, inc in next st) repeat 3 times [9]
Rnd 3 – 5: sc in all 9 st [9]
Rnd 6: (sc in next st, dec) repeat 3 times [6]
Slst in next st. Fasten off, leaving a long tail for sewing. The fins don't need to be stuffed. Sew the fins to the sides of the body, over rounds 10-11, with an interspace of 9 stitches across the belly ❽.

Materials
Sport weight yarn in
- Yellow (9 grams)
- Brown (4 grams)
- White (leftover)
- Black (leftover)

B-1 / 2.5 mm crochet hook
Yarn needle
Pins
Scissors
Stitch markers
Fiberfill for stuffing

Size
2.4" / 6 cm long when made with the indicated yarn

Skills needed
magic ring *(page 17)*
crocheting in front and back loops only *(page 14)*
half double crochet *(page 15)*
crocheting in rows *(page 11)*

DO YOU WANT TO MAKE A CHENILLE LION?

Materials:
Chenille super bulky weight yarn in
- Yellow (27 grams)
- Brown (12 grams)
- White (9 grams)
- Black (leftover)

H-8 / 5 mm crochet hook

Size:
This will result in a 6" / 15 cm long lion

Scan or visit **www.amigurumi.com/5419** to share pictures and find inspiration in our gallery.

TOTO THE LION

Toto is a bird-watcher at heart. He loves sitting underneath his favorite tree, listening to the cheerful birdsong all around him while trying to guess how many birds he can hear. A little sparrow keeps him company through-out the day, chirping boldly and making him laugh. His best friend Nora the Hippo made Toto a Bird Bingo Card and he only needs to spot 2 more bird species before he can roar 'Bingo!'.

1

2

3

4

HEAD AND BODY *(in yellow yarn)*

Rnd 1: start 6 sc in a magic ring [6]
Rnd 2: inc in all 6 st [12]
Rnd 3: (sc in next st, inc in next st) repeat 6 times [18]
Mark the 5th and 14th stitch of round 3 with a stitch marker.
Rnd 4: (sc in next 2 st, inc in next st) repeat 6 times [24]
Rnd 5: (sc in next 7 st, inc in next st) repeat 3 times [27]
Rnd 6: sc in all 27 st [27]
Rnd 7: BLO sc in all 27 st [27]
Rnd 8 – 14: sc in all 27 st [27]
With black yarn, embroider the eyes on rounds 3-4, using the marked stitches as a guide 1.
Rnd 15: (sc in next 7 st, dec) repeat 3 times [24]
Rnd 16: (sc in next 2 st, dec) repeat 6 times [18]
Stuff the head and body with fiberfill and continue stuffing as you go.
Rnd 17: (sc in next st, dec) repeat 6 times [12]
Rnd 18: dec 6 times [6]
Fasten off, leaving a yarn tail. Using your yarn needle, weave the yarn tail through the front loop of each remaining stitch and pull it tight to close. Weave in the yarn end.

MANE *(in brown yarn)*

Since you worked round 7 of the body in the back loops only, you can now use the front loops to create the mane. Pull up a loop of brown yarn in the first leftover front loop on round 7 of the body 2 and make a slst.
Rnd 1: (sc + hdc + hdc + sc in next st, slst in next st) repeat 13 times [65] 3
Fasten off, leaving a yarn tail. Take the yarn tail on a yarn needle, bring it through the first sc of round 1 and weave in the yarn end 4.

5 6 7 8

SNOUT *(in white yarn)*

Rnd 1: start 6 sc in a magic ring [6]
Rnd 2: (sc in next st, inc in next st) repeat 3 times [9]
Fasten off, leaving a long tail for sewing. With black yarn, embroider a nose on the snout between rounds 1 and 2. The nose is 2 stitches wide. Embroider a vertical stripe over round 1 below the nose. Sew the snout onto the head, centered over the magic ring, with the top positioned just below round 2 and the bottom just above round 4, right between the eyes.

EAR *(make 2, in yellow yarn)*

Rnd 1: start 6 sc in a magic ring [6]
Rnd 2: sc in all 6 st [6]
Slst in next st. Fasten off, leaving a long tail for sewing. The ears don't need to be stuffed. Flatten the ear and sew the bottom side closed with a few stitches 5. Sew the ears to round 6 of the head, with an interspace of 7 stitches.

LEG *(make 4, in yellow yarn)*

Rnd 1: start 4 sc in a magic ring [4]
Rnd 2: (sc in next st, inc in next st) repeat 2 times [6]
Fasten off, leaving a long tail for sewing. Sew the legs to the bottom of the body. Sew the front legs over rounds 9-10, with an interspace of 4 stitches across the belly. Sew the hind legs over rounds 14-15, with an interspace of 3 stitches across the belly.

TAIL *(in yellow yarn)*

Ch 6. Crochet in rows.
Row 1: start in second ch from hook, sc in next 5 ch [5]
Fasten off, leaving a long tail for sewing. Cut 4 strands of brown yarn, each about 4 inches / 10 cm in length, and fold them 2 by 2. Insert your crochet hook in the outer stitch of the tail 6 and pull the strands halfway through the stitch. Pull the yarn tails through the loop 7 and make a knot. Trim the yarn to the desired length 8. Sew the tail to the back of the body, on round 15.

Materials
Sport weight yarn in
  White (8 grams)
  Black (8 grams)
B-1 / 2.5 mm crochet hook
Safety eyes (7 mm)
Yarn needle
Pins
Scissors
Stitch markers
Fiberfill for stuffing

Size
3" / 8 cm long when made with the indicated yarn

Skills needed
magic ring *(page 17)*
changing color *(page 20)*
fastening off invisible join *(page 19)*

DO YOU WANT TO MAKE A CHENILLE PANDA?

Materials:
Chenille super bulky weight yarn in
  White (24 grams)
  Black (24 grams)
H-8 / 5 mm crochet hook
Safety eyes (14 mm)

Size:
This will result in a 7.8" / 20 cm long panda

Scan or visit **www.amigurumi.com/5420** to share pictures and find inspiration in our gallery.

TOMO THE PANDA

While Tomo the Panda was already well-known for his long naps and late mornings, his recent passion for making desserts has everyone talking. From sticky rice cakes to bamboo-flavored pastries, Tomo can make it all, and he'll happily share it with his friends. The desserts always work out – as long as he doesn't fall asleep while they're in the oven, of course!

EYE SPOT *(make 2, in black yarn)*

Rnd 1: start 8 sc in a magic ring [8]
Fasten off with an invisible join. Insert the safety eye through the magic ring, but don't close the washer yet ❶.

HEAD AND BODY *(start in white yarn)*

Rnd 1: start 6 sc in a magic ring [6]
Rnd 2: inc in all 6 st [12]
Rnd 3: (sc in next st, inc in next st) repeat 6 times [18]
Mark the 5th and 13th stitch of round 3 with a stitch marker.
Rnd 4: (sc in next 2 st, inc in next st) repeat 6 times [24]
Rnd 5: sc in all 24 st [24]
Rnd 6: (sc in next 3 st, inc in next st) repeat 6 times [30]
Rnd 7 – 10: sc in all 30 st [30]
Position the eye spots on the head, between rounds 3 and 4, and insert the safety eyes in the stitches you marked earlier ❷. Close the washers, but don't sew the eye spots to the head yet.
Rnd 11: (sc in next 3 st, dec) repeat 6 times [24]
Rnd 12: (sc in next st, dec) repeat 8 times [16]
Rnd 13: sc in all 16 st [16]
Change to black yarn.
Rnd 14: (sc in next 3 st, inc in next st) repeat 4 times [20]
Rnd 15: sc in all 20 st [20]
Stuff the head and body with fiberfill and continue stuffing as you go.
Rnd 16: (sc in next 4 st, inc in next st) repeat 4 times [24]
Change to white yarn.
Rnd 17 – 19: sc in all 24 st [24]
Rnd 20: (sc in next 2 st, dec) repeat 6 times [18]
Rnd 21: (sc in next st, dec) repeat 6 times [12]
Rnd 22: dec 6 times [6]
Fasten off, leaving a yarn tail. Using your yarn needle, weave the yarn tail through the front loop of each remaining stitch and pull it tight to close. Weave in the yarn end. Sew the eye spots to the head.

SNOUT *(in white yarn)*

Rnd 1: start 6 sc in a magic ring [6]
Rnd 2: inc in all 6 st [12]
Rnd 3: sc in all 12 st [12]
Slst in next st. Fasten off, leaving a long tail for sewing. With black yarn, embroider the nose between

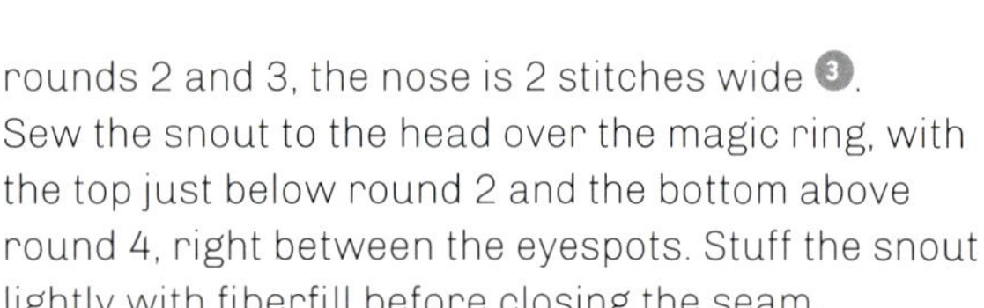

rounds 2 and 3, the nose is 2 stitches wide ❸. Sew the snout to the head over the magic ring, with the top just below round 2 and the bottom above round 4, right between the eyespots. Stuff the snout lightly with fiberfill before closing the seam.

EAR *(make 2, in black yarn)*

Rnd 1: start 6 sc in a magic ring [6]
Rnd 2: (sc in next st, inc in next st) repeat 3 times [9]
Rnd 3: sc in all 9 st [9]
Slst in next st. Fasten off, leaving a long tail for sewing. The ears don't need to be stuffed. Flatten the ears. Sew the ears on round 8 of the head, with an interspace of 6 stitches.

FRONT LEG *(make 2, in black yarn)*

Rnd 1: start 6 sc in a magic ring [6]
Rnd 2: (sc in next st, inc in next st) repeat 3 times [9]
Rnd 3 – 4: sc in all 9 st [9]
Rnd 5: (sc in next st, dec) repeat 3 times [6]
Rnd 6 – 7: sc in all 6 st [6]
Slst in next st. Fasten off, leaving a long tail for sewing. Stuff the front legs lightly with fiberfill. Sew the legs to round 15 of the body, with an interspace of 5 stitches across the belly.

HIND LEG *(make 2, in black yarn)*

Rnd 1: start 6 sc in a magic ring [6]
Rnd 2: (sc in next st, inc in next st) repeat 3 times [9]
Rnd 3 – 5: sc in all 9 st [9]
Rnd 6: (sc in next st, dec) repeat 3 times [6]
Slst in next st. Fasten off, leaving a long tail for sewing. The hind legs don't need to be stuffed. Sew the legs to round 20 of the body, with an interspace of 4 stitches across the belly ❹.

TAIL *(in white yarn)*

Rnd 1: start 6 sc in a magic ring [6]
Slst in next st. Fasten off, leaving a long tail for sewing. Sew the tail to the back of the body, on round 21.

OLIVER THE MOUSE

You'll never meet a mouse who loves peanuts more than Oliver. He can sniff out his favorite nuts wherever they're hidden, whether it's in a pantry jar or in a discarded snack wrapper underneath a park bench. He stores his prized stash in his burrow, and each night, he happily nibbles a few nuts, dreaming of a world where we could all savor delicacies such as peanut soup and peanut pizza.

Materials
Sport weight yarn in
  Brown (12 grams)
  Beige (4 grams)
B-1 / 2.5 mm crochet hook
Safety eyes (7 mm)
Yarn needle
Pins
Scissors
Stitch markers
Fiberfill for stuffing

Size
2.4" / 6 cm tall when made with the indicated yarn

Skills needed
magic ring *(page 17)*
crocheting in rows *(page 11)*
fastening off invisible join *(page 19)*

DO YOU WANT TO MAKE A CHENILLE MOUSE?

Materials:
Chenille super bulky weight yarn in
  Brown (36 grams)
  Beige (12 grams)
H-8 / 5 mm crochet hook
Safety eyes (15 mm)

Size:
This will result in a 6.3" / 16 cm tall mouse

Scan or visit **www.amigurumi.com/5421** to share pictures and find inspiration in our gallery.

HEAD AND BODY *(in brown yarn)*

Rnd 1: start 6 sc in a magic ring [6]
Rnd 2: inc in all 6 st [12]
Rnd 3: (sc in next st, inc in next st) repeat 6 times [18]
Rnd 4: (sc in next 2 st, inc in next st) repeat 6 times [24]
Rnd 5: (sc in next 3 st, inc in next st) repeat 6 times [30]
Rnd 6 – 7: sc in all 30 st [30]
Rnd 8: (sc in next 4 st, inc in next st) repeat 6 times [36]
Rnd 9 – 10: sc in all 36 st [36]
Insert the safety eyes between rounds 8-9, with an interspace of 6 stitches.
Rnd 11: (sc in next 4 st, dec) repeat 6 times [30]
Rnd 12: (sc in next 3 st, dec) repeat 6 times [24]
Rnd 13: (sc in next st, dec) repeat 8 times [16]
Rnd 14: sc in all 16 st [16]
Stuff the head and body with fiberfill and continue stuffing as you go.
Rnd 15: (sc in next st, inc in next st) repeat 8 times [24]
Rnd 16 – 17: sc in all 24 st [24]
Rnd 18: (sc in next st, dec) repeat 8 times [16]
Rnd 19: dec 8 times [8]
Fasten off, leaving a yarn tail. Using your yarn needle, weave the yarn tail through the front loop of each remaining stitch and pull it tight to close. Weave in the yarn end.

SNOUT *(in brown yarn)*

Rnd 1: start 6 sc in a magic ring [6]
Rnd 2: (sc in next st, inc in next st) repeat 3 times [9]
Slst in next st. Fasten off, leaving a long tail for sewing. With beige yarn, embroider the nose on round 1 of the snout ❶ ❷ ❸. Sew the snout between rounds 8 and 12 of the head.

EAR *(make 2, in brown yarn)*

Rnd 1: start 6 sc in a magic ring [6]
Rnd 2: inc in all 6 st [12]
Rnd 3: (sc in next 2 st, inc in next 2 st, sc in next 2 st) repeat 2 times [16]
Rnd 4 – 5: sc in all 16 st [16]
Rnd 6: (sc in next 2 st, dec 2 times, sc in next 2 st) repeat 2 times [12]
Slst in next st. Fasten off, leaving a long tail for sewing. The ears don't need to be stuffed. Flatten the ears ❹.

INSIDE EAR *(make 2, in beige yarn)*

Rnd 1: start 8 sc in a magic ring [8]
Fasten off with an invisible join and weave in the yarn end. Position the inside ears in the middle of the outer ears and sew them on. Sew the ears to rounds 4-7 of the head, with an interspace of 6 stitches.

FRONT LEG *(make 2, in brown yarn)*

Rnd 1: start 6 sc in a magic ring [6]
Fasten off, leaving a long tail for sewing. Sew the front legs to the front of the body, between rounds 17-18.

HIND LEG *(make 2, in brown yarn)*

Rnd 1: start 6 sc in a magic ring [6]
Rnd 2: (sc in next st, inc in next st) repeat 3 times [9]
Fasten off, leaving a long tail for sewing. Sew the hind legs to the body, over rounds 16-18, right next to the front legs.

TAIL *(in beige yarn)*

Ch 17. Crochet in rows.
Row 1: start in second ch from hook, slst in next 16 ch [16]
Fasten off, leaving a long tail for sewing. Sew the tail to the back of the body, between rounds 16 and 17.

Materials
Sport weight yarn in
- Black (16 grams)
- Yellow (leftover)
- White (4 grams)
- Orange (leftover)

B-1 / 2.5 mm crochet hook
Safety eyes (8 mm)
Yarn needle
Pins
Scissors
Stitch markers
Fiberfill for stuffing

Size
2.7" / 7 cm tall when made with the indicated yarn

Skills needed
magic ring *(page 17)*
changing color *(page 20)*
crocheting around a foundation chain *(page 18)*
joining parts – crocheting pieces together *(page 22)*

DO YOU WANT TO MAKE A CHENILLE TOUCAN?

Materials:
Chenille super bulky weight yarn in
- Black (48 grams)
- Yellow (6 grams)
- White (12 grams)
- Orange (6 grams)

H-8 / 5 mm crochet hook
Safety eyes (16 mm)

Size:
This will result in a 5.1" / 13 cm tall toucan

Scan or visit **www.amigurumi.com/5422** to share pictures and find inspiration in our gallery.

TONY THE TOUCAN

Tony the Toucan can't resist a water fountain. Every evening, he flies down to the town square, perching near the sparkling sprays. With a big swoop, he dips his beak into the water, enjoying the cool sensation of the droplets sliding down. Children who're playing nearby often giggle and toss him some tasty breadcrumbs. After a long day's work, you really have to choose whatever makes you feel refreshed.

FACE PATCH *(in white yarn)*

Ch 6. Stitches are worked around both sides of the foundation chain.

Rnd 1: start in second ch from hook, sc in next 4 st, 3 sc in next st. Continue on the other side of the foundation chain, sc in next 3 st, inc in last st [12]

Rnd 2: (inc in next st, sc in next 3 st, inc in next 2 st) repeat 2 times [18]

Rnd 3: sc in next st, inc in next st, sc in next 3 st, (sc in next st, inc in next st) repeat 3 times, sc in next 3 st, (sc in next st, inc in next st) repeat 2 times [24]

Rnd 4: sc in next 2 st, inc in next st, sc in next 3 st, (sc in next st, inc in next st) repeat 2 times, sc in next st, (sc in next st, inc in next st) repeat 2 times, sc in next 3 st, (sc in next st, inc in next st) repeat 2 times, sc in next 2 st [31]

Rnd 5: inc in next st, sc in next st, slst in next st [4]

Leave the remaining stitches unworked.

Fasten off, leaving a long tail for sewing.

HEAD AND BODY *(in black yarn)*

Rnd 1: start 6 sc in a magic ring [6]

Rnd 2: inc in all 6 st [12]

Rnd 3: (sc in next st, inc in next st) repeat 6 times [18]

Rnd 4: (sc in next 2 st, inc in next st) repeat 6 times [24]

Rnd 5: sc in all 24 st [24]

Rnd 6: (sc in next 3 st, inc in next st) repeat 6 times [30]

Rnd 7 – 10: sc in all 30 st [30]

Rnd 11: (sc in next 4 st, inc in next st) repeat 6 times [36]

Rnd 12 – 15: sc in all 36 st [36]

Rnd 16: (sc in next 4 st, dec) repeat 6 times [30]

Rnd 17: (sc in next 3 st, dec) repeat 6 times [24]

Pin and sew the face patch between rounds 4 and 13 of the head.

Insert the safety eyes between rounds 2-3 of the face patch and through the corresponding rounds of the head ❶ ❷, with an interspace of 6 stitches. Close the washers.

Stuff the head and body with fiberfill and continue stuffing as you go.

Rnd 18: (sc in next 2 st, dec) repeat 6 times [18]
Rnd 19: (sc in next st, dec) repeat 6 times [12]
Rnd 20: dec 6 times [6]
Fasten off, leaving a yarn tail. Using your yarn needle, weave the yarn tail through the front loop of each remaining stitch and pull it tight to close. Weave in the yarn end.

BEAK *(start in black yarn)*

Rnd 1: start 6 sc in a magic ring [6]
Rnd 2: sc in next st, inc in next 3 st, sc in next 2 st [9]
Change to orange yarn.
Rnd 3 – 4: sc in all 9 st [9]
Change to yellow yarn.
Rnd 5 – 7: sc in all 9 st [9]
Slst in next st. Fasten off, leaving a long tail for sewing. Stuff the beak lightly with fiberfill. Sew the beak between the eyes.

WING *(make 2, in black yarn)*

Rnd 1: start 6 sc in a magic ring [6]
Rnd 2: (sc in next st, inc in next st) repeat 3 times [9]
Rnd 3 – 4: sc in all 9 st [9]
Rnd 5: (sc in next st, dec) repeat 3 times [6]
Rnd 6: (sc in next st, dec) repeat 2 times [4]
Fasten off, leaving a long tail for sewing. The wings don't need to be stuffed. Using your yarn needle, weave the yarn tail through the front loop of each remaining stitch and pull it tight to close, leaving a long tail for sewing. Sew the wings to the sides of the body, at an angle, with the top of the wings on round 9 and the bottom of the wings on round 13. The tip of the wings is pointing towards the back of the body. Sew all around the wings, but leave the tip unsewn.

TAIL *(in black yarn)*

We start by making 3 tail feathers (1 large and 2 small feathers), which we'll later join together to make the tail.

Large feather *(in black yarn)*

Rnd 1: start 6 sc in a magic ring [6]
Rnd 2 – 3: sc in all 6 st [6]
Slst in next st. Fasten off and weave in the yarn end.

Small feather *(make 2, in black yarn)*

Rnd 1: start 5 sc in a magic ring [5]
Rnd 2: sc in all 5 st [5]
Slst in next st. Fasten off and weave in the yarn end on the first small feather. Don't fasten off on the second small feather. In the next round, we'll join the feathers together to create the tail.

Joining the feathers

Note: The Toucan's tail is identical to the Cockatoo's tail. You can find step pictures on page 101.
Rnd 3: sc in next 3 st on the second small feather, continue in the first st of the large feather, sc in next 3 st on the large feather, continue in the first st of the first small feather, sc in next 5 st on the first small feather, continue in the fourth st of the large feather, sc in next 3 st on the large feather, continue in the fourth st of the second small feather, sc in next 2 st on the second small feather [16]
Rnd 4: (sc in next 2 st, dec) repeat 4 times [12]
Fasten off, leaving a long tail for sewing. The tail doesn't need to be stuffed. Sew the tail horizontally to the back of the body, on round 15.

Materials
Sport weight yarn in
Yellow (9 grams)
Pink (6 grams)
Black (leftover)
B-1 / 2.5 mm crochet hook
Yarn needle
Pins
Scissors
Stitch markers
Fiberfill for stuffing

Size
3.5" / 9 cm tall when made with the indicated yarn

Skills needed
magic ring *(page 17)*

DO YOU WANT TO MAKE A CHENILLE SNAIL?

Materials:
Chenille super bulky weight yarn in
Yellow (27 grams)
Pink (18 grams)
Black (leftover)
H-8 / 5 mm crochet hook

Size:
This will result in a 6.3" / 16 cm tall snail

Scan or visit **www.amigurumi.com/5423** to share pictures and find inspiration in our gallery.

SUZY THE SNAIL

If you have a rose bush in your garden, there's a chance that Suzy the Snail will come round to visit. She loves everything about roses: the colors, the scents, the petals that are soft to the touch (but thorns, not so much). She has a busy schedule and tries to visit a different rose garden every weekend, bringing a tiny picnic and a flask of tea with her on her outings.

HEAD AND BODY *(in yellow yarn)*

Rnd 1: start 6 sc in a magic ring [6]
Rnd 2: inc in all 6 st [12]
Rnd 3: (sc in next st, inc in next st) repeat 6 times [18]
Rnd 4: (sc in next 5 st, inc in next st) repeat 3 times [21]
Rnd 5 – 6: sc in all 21 st [21]
Rnd 7: (sc in next 5 st, dec) repeat 3 times [18]
Rnd 8: sc in all 18 st [18]
Rnd 9: (sc in next st, dec) repeat 6 times [12]
Stuff the head with fiberfill and continue stuffing the head and body as you go.
Rnd 10: (sc in next 2 st, dec) repeat 3 times [9]
Rnd 11 – 22: sc in all 9 st [9]
Rnd 23: (sc in next st, dec) repeat 3 times [6]
Fasten off, leaving a long yarn tail. Using your yarn needle, weave the yarn tail through the front loop of each remaining stitch and pull it tight to close. Leave a long tail for sewing. Weave the yarn tail to

the center top of the body and bring it out between rounds 19 and 20, so you can use it to sew the shell to the body later ❶. With black yarn, embroider the eyes slightly diagonally, over rounds 3 and 4 with an interspace of 2 stitches at the bottom ❷ ❸.

ANTENNA *(make 2, in yellow yarn)*

Rnd 1: start 5 sc in a magic ring [5]
Rnd 2: sc in all 5 st [5]
Rnd 3: sc in next 3 st, dec [4]
Fasten off, leaving a long tail for sewing. You can stuff the antenna lightly, but stuffing is optional. Sew the antennae on round 3 of the head, with an interspace of 2 stitches.

SHELL PART *(make 2, in pink yarn)*

Rnd 1: start 8 sc in a magic ring [8]
Rnd 2: inc in all 8 st [16]
Rnd 3: (sc in next st, inc in next st) repeat 8 times [24]
Rnd 4: (sc in next 3 st, inc in next st) repeat 6 times [30]
Rnd 5 – 6: sc in all 30 st [30]
Fasten off and weave in the yarn end. With yellow yarn, embroider a yellow spiral between the rounds, starting at the magic ring and ending at the end of round 5 ❹ ❺. Sew both shell parts together ❻, stuffing them with fiberfill before closing the seam. Sew the shell on top of the body, over rounds 10-18, using the yellow yarn tail of the body ❼.

Materials
Sport weight yarn in
White (7 grams)
Brown (4 grams)
Pink (leftover)
Beige (leftover)
Black (leftover)
B-1 / 2.5 mm crochet hook
Yarn needle
Pins
Scissors
Stitch markers
Fiberfill for stuffing

Size
2.4" / 6 cm long when made with the indicated yarn

Skills needed
magic ring *(page 17)*
changing color *(page 20)*
crocheting in rows *(page 11)*

DO YOU WANT TO MAKE A CHENILLE COW?

Materials:
Chenille super bulky weight yarn in
White (21 grams)
Brown (12 grams)
Pink (6 grams)
Beige (6 grams)
Black (leftover)
H-8 / 5 mm crochet hook

Size:
This will result in a 5.1" / 13 cm long cow

Scan or visit **www.amigurumi.com/5424** to share pictures and find inspiration in our gallery.

BERTHA THE COW

Meet Bertha, the water-loving cow! While the other cows prefer to lie down in the shade or leisurely stroll around to eat more grass, Bertha likes to wade into the pond, her hooves gently stirring the water. She would love to jump into the lake sometime, but she'd need swimming lessons first. Maybe Mr. Duck could help her out?

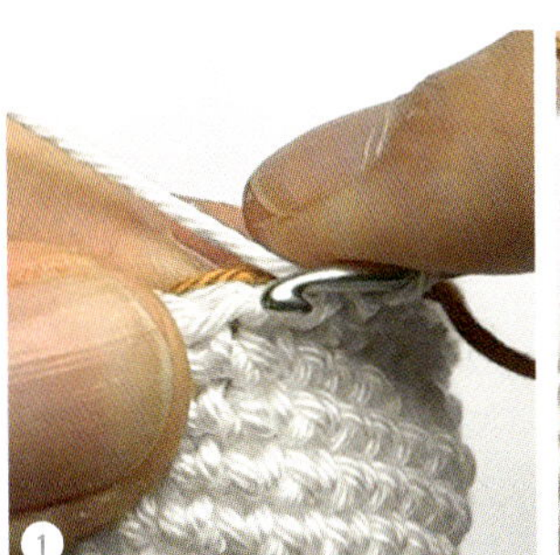

HEAD AND BODY *(start in white yarn)*

Rnd 1: start 6 sc in a magic ring [6]
Rnd 2: inc in all 6 st [12]
Rnd 3: (sc in next st, inc in next st) repeat 6 times [18]
Mark the 5th and 14th stitch of round 3 with a stitch marker.
Rnd 4: (sc in next 2 st, inc in next st) repeat 6 times [24]
Rnd 5: (sc in next 7 st, inc in next st) repeat 3 times [27]
Rnd 6 – 9: sc in all 27 st [27]
In the next rounds, we'll make the spots on the body, alternating between white and brown yarn. Change color when indicated.
Rnd 10: sc in next 20 st, (brown) 1 2 3 4 sc in next 2 st, (white) sc in next 5 st [27]
Rnd 11: sc in next 8 st, (brown) sc in next 3 st, (white) sc in next 8 st, (brown) sc in next 4 st, (white) sc in next 4 st [27]
Rnd 12: sc in next 7 st, (brown) sc in next 5 st, (white) sc in next 7 st, (brown) sc in next 4 st, (white) sc in next 4 st [27]
Rnd 13: sc in next 7 st, (brown) sc in next 5 st, (white) sc in next 8 st, (brown) sc in next 2 st, (white) sc in next 5 st [27]
Rnd 14: sc in next 7 st, (brown) dec, sc in next 3 st, (white) sc in next 4 st, dec, sc in next 7 st, dec [24]
Rnd 15: (sc in next 2 st, dec) repeat 2 times, (brown) sc in next 2 st, (white) dec, (sc in next 2 st, dec) repeat 3 times [18]
Stuff the head and body with fiberfill and continue stuffing as you go. Continue crocheting in white yarn.
Rnd 16: (sc in next st, dec) repeat 6 times [12]

Rnd 17: dec 6 times [6]
Fasten off, leaving a yarn tail. Using your yarn needle, weave the yarn tail through the front loop of each remaining stitch and pull it tight to close. Weave in the yarn end. With black yarn, embroider the eyes on rounds 3-4, using the marked stitches as a guide 5.

SNOUT *(in pink yarn)*

Rnd 1: start 6 sc in a magic ring [6]
Rnd 2: inc in all 6 st [12]
Rnd 3: sc in all 12 st [12]
Slst in next st. Fasten off, leaving a long tail for sewing. With black yarn, embroider the nostrils on round 2 of the snout 6 7. Sew the snout to the head, over the magic ring, with the top just below round 2 and the bottom above round 4, right between the eyes. Stuff the snout lightly with fiberfill before closing the seam.

EAR *(make 2, in brown yarn)*

Rnd 1: start 4 sc in a magic ring [4]
Rnd 2: (sc in next st, inc in next st) repeat 2 times [6]
Rnd 3: (sc in next 2 st, inc in next st) repeat 2 times [8]
Rnd 4: sc in all 8 st [8]
Slst in next st. Fasten off, leaving a long tail for sewing. The ears don't need to be stuffed. Flatten the ear, pinch it at the bottom and sew it with a few stitches to hold in this position 8. Sew the ears to round 7 of the head, with an interspace of 9 stitches.

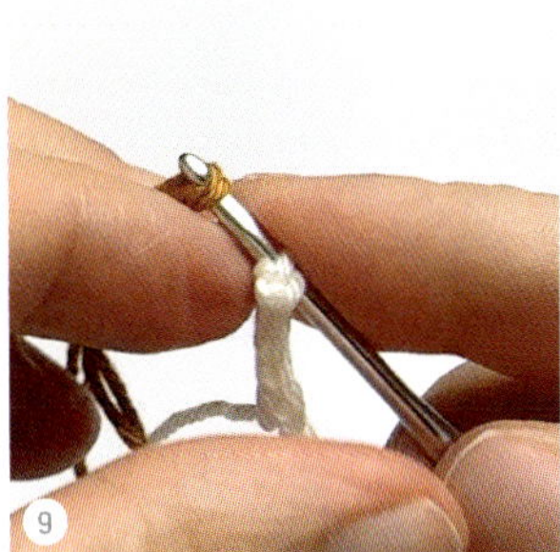
9

10

11

HORN *(make 2, in beige yarn)*

Rnd 1: start 4 sc in a magic ring [4]
Rnd 2: (sc in next st, inc in next st) repeat 2 times [6]
Slst in next st. Fasten off, leaving a long tail for sewing. Sew the horns on rounds 6 and 7, at 1 stitch from the ears.

LEG *(make 3 in brown yarn, make 1 in white yarn)*

Rnd 1: start 4 sc in a magic ring [4]
Rnd 2: (sc in next st, inc in next st) repeat 2 times [6]
Slst in next st. Fasten off, leaving a long tail for sewing. Sew the legs to the body. Sew the front legs over rounds 8-9, with an interspace of 4 stitches across the belly. Sew the hind legs over rounds 13-14, with an interspace of 3 stitches across the belly.

TAIL *(in white yarn)*

Ch 5. Crochet in rows.
Row 1: start in second ch from hook, slst in next 4 ch [4]
Fasten off, leaving a long tail for sewing. Cut 2 strands of brown yarn, about 4 inches / 10 cm in length, and fold them. Insert your crochet hook in the last stitch of the tail and pull the strands halfway through the stitch 9 10. Pull the yarn tails through the loop and make a knot 11. Trim the yarn to the desired length. Sew the tail to the back of the body, between rounds 15 and 16.

Materials
Sport weight yarn in
 Yellow (6 grams)
 Gray (8 grams)
 Orange (leftover)
 White (leftover)
B-1 / 2.5 mm crochet hook
Safety eyes (7 mm)
Yarn needle
Pins
Scissors
Stitch markers
Fiberfill for stuffing

Size
2.7" / 7 cm tall when made with the indicated yarn

Skills needed
magic ring *(page 17)*
changing color *(page 20)*
joining parts – crocheting pieces together *(page 22)*

DO YOU WANT TO MAKE A CHENILLE COCKATIEL?

Materials:
Chenille super bulky weight yarn in
 Yellow (18 grams)
 Gray (24 grams)
 Orange (6 grams)
 White (leftover)
H-8 / 5 mm crochet hook
Safety eyes (15 mm)

Size:
This will result in a 6.7" / 17 cm tall cockatiel

Scan or visit **www.amigurumi.com/5425** to share pictures and find inspiration in our gallery.

CARA THE COCKATIEL

Cara the Cockatiel is unlike any bird you've ever met. She often sneaks out of the house, flying to the nearest playground so she can play on the seesaw. One day, she borrowed a few things from her owner's workshop so she could build her own tiny seesaw at home. Now she only needs to invite Tony the Toucan over to come play with her.

HEAD AND BODY *(start in yellow yarn)*

Rnd 1: start 6 sc in a magic ring [6]
Rnd 2: inc in all 6 st [12]
Rnd 3: (sc in next st, inc in next st) repeat 6 times [18]
Rnd 4: (sc in next 2 st, inc in next st) repeat 6 times [24]
Rnd 5: sc in all 24 st [24]
Mark the 8th and 15th stitch of round 5 with a stitch marker.
Rnd 6 – 8: sc in all 24 st [24]
Insert the safety eyes between rounds 5 and 6, in the stitches you marked earlier.
Rnd 9: (sc in next 3 st, inc in next st) repeat 6 times [30]
Change to gray yarn. Stuff the head and body with fiberfill and continue stuffing as you go.
Rnd 10: sc in all 30 st [30]
Rnd 11: (sc in next 4 st, inc in next st) repeat 6 times [36]
Rnd 12 – 14: sc in all 36 st [36]
Rnd 15: (sc in next 4 st, dec) repeat 6 times [30]
Rnd 16: (sc in next 3 st, dec) repeat 6 times [24]
Rnd 17: (sc in next 2 st, dec) repeat 6 times [18]
Rnd 18: (sc in next st, dec) repeat 6 times [12]
Rnd 19: dec 6 times [6]
Fasten off, leaving a yarn tail. Using your yarn needle, weave the yarn tail through the front loop of each remaining stitch and pull it tight to close. Weave in the yarn end.
With gray yarn, embroider the beak over round 6, centered between the eyes. First sew 6-9 vertical stitches over round 6, then add a few horizontal stitches over the top of the beak (the beak is one stitch wide at the top). 1 2

CHEEK *(make 2, in orange yarn)*

Rnd 1: start 4 sc in a magic ring [4]
Slst in next st. Fasten off, leaving a long tail for sewing. Sew the cheeks to the sides of the head,

between rounds 6 and 9, right behind the eyes.

LARGE HEAD FEATHER *(in yellow yarn)*

Rnd 1: start 5 sc in a magic ring [5]
Rnd 2 – 5: sc in all 5 st [5]
Slst in next st. Fasten off, leaving a long tail for sewing. Lightly stuff the feather with fiberfill.

MEDIUM HEAD FEATHER
(in yellow yarn)

Rnd 1: start 5 sc in a magic ring [5]
Rnd 2 – 4: sc in all 5 st [5]
Slst in next st. Fasten off, leaving a long tail for sewing. Lightly stuff the feather with fiberfill.

SMALL HEAD FEATHER
(in yellow yarn)

Rnd 1: start 5 sc in a magic ring [5]
Rnd 2 – 3: sc in all 5 st [5]
Slst in next st. Fasten off, leaving a long tail for sewing. Lightly stuff the feather with fiberfill.
Sew the feathers on top of the head. The large head feather sits at the front, on round 2. The medium head feather sits just behind, covering the magic ring of the head. The small head feather sits just behind the medium head feather.

WING *(make 2, start in gray yarn)*

Rnd 1: start 6 sc in a magic ring [6]
Rnd 2: (sc in next st, inc in next st) repeat 3 times [9]
Rnd 3 – 4: sc in all 9 st [9]
Change to white yarn.
Rnd 5: (sc in next st, dec) repeat 3 times [6]
Rnd 6: (sc in next st, dec) repeat 2 times [4]
Fasten off, leaving a yarn tail. The wings don't need to be stuffed. Using your yarn needle, weave the yarn tail through the front loop of each remaining stitch and pull it tight to close. Leave a long tail for sewing. Sew the wings to the sides of the body, at an angle, with the top of the wings on round 11 and the bottom of the wings on round 14. The tip of the wings is pointing towards the back of the body. Sew all around the wings, but leave the tip unsewn.

TAIL FEATHER *(in gray yarn)*

We start by making 3 feathers, which we'll later join together to make the tail.

Large feather *(in gray yarn)*

Rnd 1: start 6 sc in a magic ring [6]
Rnd 2 – 3: sc in all 6 st [6]
Slst in next st. Fasten off and weave in the yarn end.

Small feather *(make 2, in gray yarn)*

Rnd 1: start 5 sc in a magic ring [5]
Rnd 2: sc in all 5 st [5]
Slst in next st. Fasten off and weave in the yarn end on the first feather. Don't fasten off on the second feather. In the next round, we'll join the feathers together to create the tail.

Joining the feathers

Rnd 3: sc in next 3 st on the second small feather, continue in the first st of the large feather ③, sc in next 3 st on the large feather, continue in the first st of the first small feather ④, sc in next 5 st on the first small feather, continue in the fourth st of the large feather ⑤, sc in next 3 st on the large feather, continue in the fourth st of the second small feather, sc in next 2 st on the second small feather [16] ⑥
Rnd 4: (sc in next 2 st, dec) repeat 4 times [12] ⑦
Fasten off, leaving a long tail for sewing. Stuff the tail feather lightly with fiberfill. Sew the tail feather to the bottom back of the body, on round 15 ⑧.

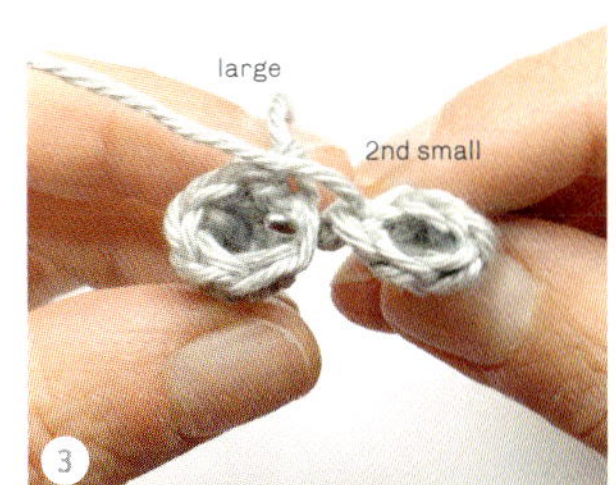

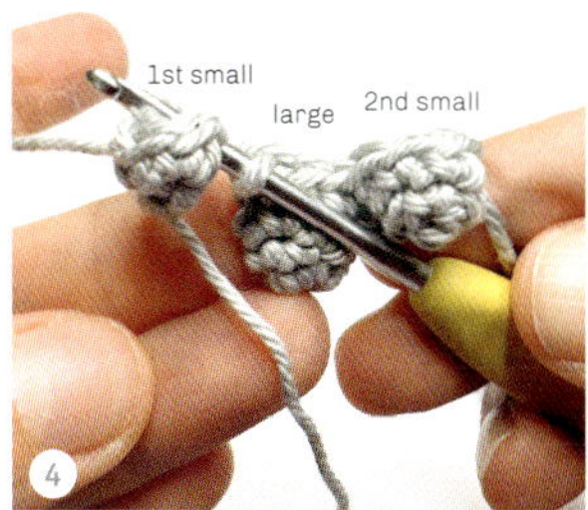

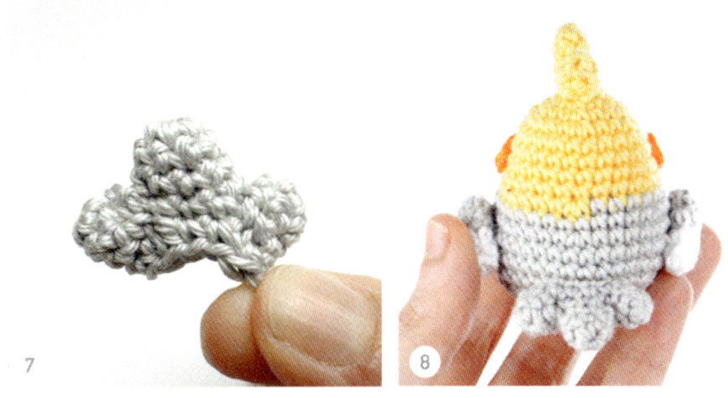

I love discovering what you make
with the patterns from my book!

Adrienn Wéber

Astrid Markman

Serena Chew

Kristi Randmaa

raquelalvescroche

Sandra Zheng

Dóra Sipos-Járási

sophielu.crochet

Sandra Belleval

Caroline Vandier

Astrid Markman

Dóra Sipos-Járási

Sandra Belleval

Debbie Eastman

Rebecca Lyon

Lutgarde van Dijck

Scan or visit **www.amigurumi.com/5400**
to share pictures of the creations you made with
patterns from this book or find inspiration in
characters made by others.

About the designer

When her two boys are at school, Mariska creates toy patterns for her brand DIY Fluffies. She started making sewing patterns in 2008 and has been making the cutest crochet patterns since 2015. Her work has been published in *'Sew Cute Creatures'* and *'Sew Cute to Cuddle'*, and was part of several editions in the *'Zoomigurumi'* series. Her first crochet book *'Amigurumi Made Easy'* is a global bestseller. She lives in Amsterdam, the Netherlands.

www.mariskavos.nl
www.amigurumi.com/shop/DIY-Fluffies/
www.etsy.com/shop/diyfluffies
instagram @diyfluffies
www.youtube.com/diyfluffies

Thank you!

I'm incredibly grateful to my husband Yannis for his unwavering support, helpful comments, and for tolerating all of the balls of yarn and amigurumi parts that inevitably take over our living space.

To my two sons, Kyan and Mylan, who're a constant source of inspiration for me. They may be a bit too old to play with the toys themselves now, but they still give me helpful feedback whenever I'm creating something new.

I am thankful to Joke, Dora and Bruno of Meteoor Books for collaborating with me on this book and for being the best crochet book publisher.

My education at the Utrecht School of Arts was instrumental and paved the way for me to pursue my passion as a full-time toy patterns designer. I feel thankful to my parents, for ensuring that I received this comprehensive education. And a special thanks to my mom, for always motivating me to follow my dreams.

I'm also deeply appreciative of all the testers who participated in this project and whose comments have polished the amigurumi patterns: Adrienn Wéber, Amy Jones, Anna Persson, Annegret Siegert, Ashton Kirkham, Astrid Markman, Barbara Roman, Bianka Karolkiewicz, Caroline Vandier, Debbie Eastman, Dóra Sipos-Járási, Elise Van den Poel, Esther van Veen, Ilonka Ladenius, Iris Dongo, Jasmijn van Binsbergen, Jill Constantine, Jimena Bouso, Karen Celestine Lee, Karina Green, Kate Waugh, Kristi Randmaa, Leeke Brandsma, Lotte Nørgaard Pedersen, Louisa Wong, Luisa Willem, Lutgarde van Dijck, Marianne Rosqvist, Mariska Van den Berg, Marleen Mertens, Nicole Schavemaker, Rebecca Lyon, Sandra Belleval, Sandra Zheng, Serena Chew, Shannon Kishbaugh, Silke Bridgman and Sonia Fox.

And lastly, I would like express my appreciation for all of my followers, pattern buyers, YouTube video watchers, and everyone else who has supported me on my journey of creating amigurumi patterns. You're the best!